MODERN HUMANITIES RESEARCH ASSOCIATION
TEXTS AND DISSERTATIONS
(formerly Dissertation Series)
VOLUME 42

Editor
DAVID HENN
(Spanish)

THE DIALECTICS OF FAITH
IN THE POETRY OF
JOSÉ BERGAMÍN

THE DIALECTICS OF FAITH
IN THE POETRY OF
JOSÉ BERGAMÍN

by
HELEN WING

Published by
W. S. MANEY & SON LTD
for the
MODERN HUMANITIES RESEARCH ASSOCIATION
1995

Published by
W. S. Maney & Son Ltd
for the
The Modern Humanities Research Association

HONORARY TREASURER, MHRA
KING'S COLLEGE, STRAND
LONDON WC2R 2LS
ENGLAND

ISBN 0 901286 58 3

1000847784

© The Modern Humanities Research Association 1995

Printed in England by
W. S. MANEY & SON LIMITED
HUDSON ROAD LEEDS

To Richard

CONTENTS

PREFACE

This book is a slightly revised version of a Ph.D. dissertation submitted to the University of Cambridge in September 1993.

I should like to thank the following for their help, support, and encouragement: Mrs Lorna Close, Professor Arthur Terry, both of whom acted as thesis supervisors for me; Professor Nigel Dennis, Dr John Jones, Dr Brian Powell, Dr Pamela Williams, Dr Seàn Allan, Richard Spencer, and Josephine and Russell Wing for their unfailing support during the long thesis years; the library staff of The University Library in Cambridge and The Brynmor Jones Library at the University of Hull, and also Juan Carlos Herguera for introducing me to the work of José Bergamín.

I am also grateful to the examiners of the dissertation, Dr Patricia McDermott and Dr Alison Sinclair, for the detailed comments and valuable suggestions they offered at the viva and subsequently. Finally, I wish to thank Dr David Henn for his precise and thorough editorial work. Any errors are entirely my own.

INTRODUCTION

The aim of this book is to show how the notion of faith functions in the poetry of José Bergamín (1895-1983). I make two general claims about Bergamín's writing. In the first place, I suggest that the notion of faith is the prime mover in Bergamín's thought and poetry. This faith is a faith in a transcendent reality that is beyond our perceptions, which are material. From the tension between the known and the unknown comes the dialectic of faith and doubt. Only this dialectic provides Bergamín with the integrity of struggle in his faith. Thus, he continually re-presents himself as an existentialist Christian. In the second place, I am concerned to show the way in which Bergamín extends the terms 'masculinity' and 'femininity' in a metaphorical way to connote what he sees as a related opposition of materialism and transcendence.

Faith is the key to Bergamín's raison d'être, for faith is the only thing that allows him to maintain a belief in transcendence in a century that equates the partial, relative perceptions of man with reality, in a century which believes that what cannot be spoken about should not be desired, cannot be imagined, and does not exist. When Wittgenstein stated in 1921 that 'what we cannot speak about we must pass over in silence',[1] Bergamín would have believed that he was talking about what we are capable of saying rather than what we should say. We have relative truth to say, the rest is unsayable. For Bergamín, Wittgenstein would have been alluding to a poetic truth: the silence of what we cannot say, the impenetrability of that, versus the silence of human understanding flying in the face of the infinite, the inarticulacy of anguish:

Y son estos dos silencios de signo contrario los que polarizan el pensamiento humano. La verdadera situación crítica del hombre. Entre la plenitud del silencio divino, henchido de voz, de palabra inaudita, de Verbo encarnado, y este otro vacío silencioso, mortal, de nuestra angustia, de nuestra desesperada esperanza, de nuestra zozobra temporal, vivimos y pensamos. Que no hay cruz sin raya para el hombre. No hay respuesta callada de Dios sin silencioso vacío interrogante humano. La mística religiosa y la poesía nos han mostrado y demostrado muy a las claras, a las claras celestes, todo esto. Enseñándonos a que le hagamos hueco con nuestro silencio al silencio divino; pues por eso suena nuestra voz - que es nuestra personalidad profunda - o su expresión: porque es la máscara en nosotros de lo divino; la palabra, enmascaradora en nosotros, del silencio de Dios.[2]

In the second place, whilst the language of Bergamín's desire reflects the existentialist struggle of his belief, it also suffers the tyranny of masculinity. This he feels implicitly and acts out in his poetry, leaving a customary mark of interrogation around what he does not know how to say but wants to say. He implicitly acknowledges Cixous's observation:

But we must make no mistake: men and women are caught up in a web of age-old cultural determinations that are almost unanalyzable in their complexity. One can no more speak of 'woman' than of 'man' without being trapped within an ideological theater where the proliferation of representations, images, reflections, myths, identifications, transform, deform, constantly change everyone's Imaginary and invalidate in advance any conceptualization.[3]

Language, retaining the structures of essentialism, is materialistic according to Bergamín. I shall argue that despite its illusory claims to universal objectivity, Bergamín's language struggles in the snare of phallocentrism and that it is in his poetry that Bergamín implicitly plays out the tragedy of such entrapment.

Bergamín's sense of transcendence differs from the conventional logocentrism of essentialism, for his reality, rather than being fundamental to this, the material world, requires a spiritual as well as bodily resurrection beyond it. He believes faith to be a feminine principle, opposed to the masculinity of rationality. Therefore he affirms that we are estranged or exiled from God because our linguistic tools have created objectification from our material world, which means we perceive ourselves as separate from others and separate from God. He uses his poetry as a form of reconciliation by striving for faith in the feminine; striving for doubt, fluidity, and con-fusion as against certainty, death, and reason. His vision of faith is one in which reconciliation is the opposite of exile.

The reason I wish to describe Bergamín's struggle with reality and language is because, like that of Cixous and Kafka, his is both noble and terrifying: 'To run against the window and, weak after exerting all one's strength, to step over the window sill through the splintered wood and glass.'[4]

NOTES

1 Ludwig Wittgenstein, *Tractatus Logico-Philosophicus*, trans. by D.F. Pears and B.F. McGuinness, with an introduction by Bertrand Russell (London: Routledge and Kegan Paul, 1974), p. 74.

2 José Bergamín, 'La callada de Dios', in *'Cruz y Raya': Antología*, ed. by José Bergamín (Madrid: Turner, 1974), p. 420.

3 Hélène Cixous, 'Sorties: Out and Out: Attacks/Ways Out/Forays', in Hélène Cixous and Catherine Clément, *The Newly Born Woman*, trans. by Betsy Wing, Theory and History of Literature, 24 (Manchester: Manchester University Press, 1986), pp. 63-132 (p. 83).

4 Franz Kafka, *The Diaries of Franz Kafka 1910-1923*, ed. by Max Brod (Harmondsworth: Penguin, 1972), p. 153.

CHAPTER 1

BERGAMÍN AND THE TWIN QUEST FOR IDENTITY AND IMMORTALITY

IMMORTALITY

This opening chapter aims to set the scene of the critical perspective in which Bergamín's work has been understood to date. My main contention is, as it will be throughout this study, that Bergamín's Catholicism has become such a cliché as to seem almost invisible to the critic. Consequently, Bergamín is judged, when he is judged as a writer, as someone who wants to attain literary immortality rather than Christian immortality. I maintain that he is being misread because his writing is not being looked upon as a religious act.

Crucial to this misapprehension is the problem of personality. Critics tend to confuse Bergamín's notion of personhood with his own personality, the consequences of which can be seen in the personality cult built around him. The critics' notion of personality is a twentieth-century reduction to materialist notions of literary worthiness, whereas Bergamín's notion of personhood is to do with a Christian Existentialism which focuses not on this world but on the achievement of an elision of what he considers to be a false distinction between the finite and the infinite, and self and otherness. According to Bergamín, all writing is a religious act, a realignment and an existential refocusing upon the quest for immortality.

Criticism to date on Bergamín has suffered in general from a problem of definition, torn as it is between producing an *apologia pro vita sua* and a critical appreciation of Bergamín's writing. The most recently published book on Bergamín can be no more explicit in its title than *José Bergamín*, focused as it is on a personality cult which threatens to undermine the serious study of Bergamín as a writer.[1]

In *José Bergamín*, Antonio Garrigues Díaz-Cañabate tries to define Bergamín through that which cannot be retained, documented, analysed, or refuted: his conversation. He witnesses Bergamín in an unassailable, though continually diminishing, way. He prizes above all Bergamín's conversation which, though described as 'inoubliable', is unrecorded, and of course infinitely forgettable:

Je pense qu'humainement parlant son oeuvre la plus importante aura été, avec la création de *Cruz y Raya*, la façon dont il pratiquait l'amitié: sa conversation. Dialogue avec lui si humain, si '*divertente*' comme disent les italiens, si vivant, profond, inoubliable.[2]

With this approach to Bergamín, Antonio Garrigues Díaz-Cañabate is gesturing to a more fundamental problem in the study of Bergamín which is rooted in a confusion around the notion of personhood. The personality cult that has built up around Bergamín is a critical phenomenon which arises automatically from the content of Bergamín's writings, a critical reaction to a literary persona whose subtext is that of a threatened identity. Bergamín's concern with identity, personhood, so typical of his era, and which we will come to see as a crucial preoccupation for him, is reflected in the critic's own fascination and difficulty with the person of Bergamín. Certainly Florence Delay capitulates in the struggle for definition, as she admits in her introductory note: 'L'emprise de Bergamín nous paraît autant fondée sur sa personne et ses prises de position que sur son oeuvre. C'est pourquoi nous tentons ici leur portrait conjoint' (p. 9).

It is clear that Bergamín's apologists are driven by a desire to right the wrong of what is perceived as Bergamín's vital and literary marginalization. And few are as perspicacious as Carlos Gurméndez when he alludes to Bergamín's collusion in such marginalization:

La figura de Bergamín no está marginada, y eso lo he discutido con él; él ha sido siempre un hombre muy importante, literaria y políticamente y esa es una versión que él inventó de sí mismo, aquí, en Francia y en América. 'Yo soy un esqueleto vivo, un fantasma deprimido': eso es una autoproducción suya, y la gente ha creído esos mitos que él mismo ha creado.[3]

However, Bergamín's insistence upon defining himself as an 'esqueleto vivo, un fantasma deprimido' is not simply a whimsical self-stylization. He perceives himself as an identity under threat not because of his palpable literary marginalization but rather because of his mortality. It will become apparent in this study that Bergamín has a problem with the figure of 'un hombre importante' in a much more fundamental way than Gurméndez realizes. For Bergamín is concerned with the transcendence of his mortality, his humanity and, in the symbolic order, with the intransigence of his manliness. Apparently condemned, therefore, to a partial vision of existence he feels denied the re-creative, eternalizing potential of otherness in its most fundamental sense, that of the divine.

CREDENCE TO CREED

What I consider to be the critical blindness towards Bergamín's understanding of personhood or identity is rooted in a fundamental inability to give credence to the Christian orientation of his writings. When critics do acknowledge such an orientation it frequently takes the form of an apology or a justification, a tonal feature which ultimately tends to undermine the critics' appreciative intent. Indeed, critics of Bergamín in general, like Gurméndez, customarily shy away from in-depth analyses of Bergamín's religious views. The lack of credence given to Bergamín's religious attitudes was informed originally, however, by the historical situation of the Second Republic when anticlericalism was at its peak in Spain. The continuing urge to justify reverence to Bergamín is one of the products of the long history of controversy surrounding his figure, sparked originally in the turbulent years preceding and during the Spanish Civil War.

It was during this period that Bergamín first adopted the thought-provoking stance of a Republican Catholic, which he purveyed as editor of *Cruz y Raya*.[4] As Nigel Dennis documents, Bergamín's stance was frequently viewed as either politically compromised and dangerously right wing, or ideologically inconsistent:

The presence on the Spanish cultural scene of a *Catholic* journal prepared to express *political* opinions would give rise to persistent misunderstandings of the kind that characterize Sánchez Barbudo's dismissal of *Cruz y Raya* as a 'publicación fascista'.[5]

Indeed, the most emotionally charged defences of Bergamín depict him as a lone voice under attack by the 'thought-police' of both reactionary and revolutionary forces. Nigel Dennis clarifies the political issues at stake in the general vilification of Bergamín as a left-wing Catholic in a period of Spanish history which could not cope with complex political messages such as those he espoused. Critics of all political shades attacked him as treacherous. The newness and, to some extent, the perceived naivety of Bergamín's ideas made his fellow Spaniards suspicious of his motives.[6]

Even Dennis's approach to Bergamín's political complexity draws upon his stature as a political personality which, however laudatory, still fails to give intellectual credence to Bergamín's religious orientation. His analysis of Bergamín's alignment with the social values of Marxism, for instance, is couched in terms of awe:

Such a declaration may sound rather bland in the 1980s when the dialogue between Marxists and Christians enjoys a sound base in many parts of the world; but in 1935, in a country still dominated by an arch-conservative Catholic hierarchy, it must have taken *considerable courage* to make it publicly in this way. For right-wing politicians and clerics in Spain, Marxism was at that time a terrifying threat and - as the Civil War would show -

they were prepared to go to any lengths to eradicate the danger it was seen to pose. Bergamín, to say the least, was sticking his neck out by giving his public blessing to this element of social protest contained in Marxism. (p.174, my italics)

So, for Dennis, Bergamín's radical Catholicism casts him as both a heroic revolutionary and a saint: he shows his 'considerable courage' as, alone against the Church and the right, who were prepared to go to 'any lengths' to stop Marxism in its tracks, he gives 'his public blessing' to his radical creed. Though Dennis goes a long way towards underpinning Bergamín's historical, political importance, he sidesteps any serious evaluation of his world view in particular relation to his preoccupation with divinity.

The critical confusion around the figure of Bergamín is to some extent a phenomenon which Bergamín himself was keen to promote, and yet the confusion he espouses is not the same one that the critics, in general, appear to discern. Critics who revere Bergamín the man, the political and literary personality, over Bergamín the religious artist seem to use Bergamín's enigmatic, worldly personality to excuse and to implicitly devalue the perceived quirkiness of his writings. In contrast, although Bergamín himself would draw no easy distinction between his personality and his work, between life and art, his confusion of these arenas is based on the conviction that the notion of personhood or identity intimately connects life and art. In turn, identity is intimately linked with Bergamín's notion of divinity.

So, whereas a critic such as Dennis may see in Bergamín an oppositional, political figure whose personality is his greatest asset, Bergamín's own interest in personhood is one which sees identity as the font of creative thought. Yet this is a font which is opposed to the critic's notions of personality in that the ultimate quest of Bergamín is not to shore up earthly personal gain in terms of becoming a historical personality, but rather to use the processes of identity as a way of eliding the separate nature of personhood and of merging the finite with the infinite, with the divine. Bergamín's concept of personhood is in this sense the reverse of that ordinarily expressed by critical opinion in that it militates against definition in materialistic terms. This is why Bergamín refers to himself in ways which both deny and confirm his mortality, his humanity: he sees himself as dead and yet still vital, as an 'esqueleto vivo, un fantasma deprimido'. For Bergamín, death is a two-pronged sword: it both defines humanity as mortal and annihilates identity. Bergamín wants to challenge death by seeking immortality and an identity which need not be defined in terms of the defining limit of individual mortality.

Bergamín's urge to immortality, since it is read in Christian terms, leads him to identify with Christ. The symbol of Christ merges the concepts of humanity and divinity, and the crucifixion enacts a process of becoming-through-annihilation in which Bergamín delights. His evasion of material reality, of personal and linguistic definition, becomes comprehensible only when it is regarded from a Christian perspective. Bergamín's Christian ideal is precisely that of merging the human with the divine.

It is only Giorgio Agamben who has sensed Bergamín's delectation at being the figure under attack, a mortified Christ, fascinated by the contemplation of his own pain. Indeed, every last area of his life and work (ultimately itself a false differentiation) is tinged with a sense of martyrdom, self-sacrifice, ritual mortification, and the contemplation of pain, all of which Agamben rightly associates with the baroque:

A la fois le devenir soi-même, l'ad-venir de l'oeuvre d'art et le procès de sa mortification convergent vers un unique *topos* parfaitement allégorisé dans une limite infernale ou divine, et la topologie de l'art en vient à s'identifier nécessairement à une théorie des limites. Cette idée d'une mortification critique de l'oeuvre et du double jeu de son autodissolution et de sa résurrection explique aussi en partie le rapport profond qui lie Bergamín au monde de l'allégorie théâtrale baroque, ce qui est bien plus qu'une simple affinité ou qu'une heureuse rencontre.[7]

Bergamín's artistic 'devenir soi-même', his identification with Christ, is an identification with the agonizing figure of Christ, an emptying of Self through sacrament/sacrifice, which is ultimately, through faith, a process of continual renewal. It is this identity with Christ which best expresses Bergamín's vision of personhood as a Christian process of becoming. Christ, for Bergamín, and especially the image of the crucified Christ, resides at what Agamben calls the 'limite infernale ou divine' which straddles the human and the divine. Christ's actual and symbolic status as the creator or catalyst of eternal life fuses, as far as Bergamín is concerned, the vital realm of human experience with the artistic realm. Bergamín's attitudes to life and art converge in the same way that the Christian experience merges experience and expression in the reality and image of Christ. Life becomes a quest for transcendence through the contemplation of the process of the agony of death and desired self-renewal.

THE DIALECTICS OF FAITH

Consequently, for Bergamín life is a dynamic Christian process, a dialectics of faith. Consciousness of death and the wish not to die create for him what appears to be a paradoxical notion of identity. In order not to die, in order to gain eternal life one has to relinquish one's humanity. By this I mean one has to relinquish mortality, the death which defines and limits the human. One has also to fly in the face of rationality, one has to deny death and forsake the material definitions of human identity. Thus, according to Bergamín's logic, true human existence, which would be a Christian ideal, implies the suspension of one's material sense of being in the world:

La existencia humana es esta suspensión del ser fuera de sí mismo, o mejor dicho, fuera de su razón, de su razón de ser frente a la nada. Porque este enfurecimiento trágico le suspende y adentra en la nada misma. Ser, para el metafísico de la angustia, como para los trágicos griegos, ¿es dejar de ser? Entrar en la nada, enterarse de ella, anonadarse.[8]

This 'suspensión del ser fuera de sí mismo' is not, however, merely a leap of faith for Bergamín. Since it involves the annihilation of selfhood and the denial of one's sense perceptions, in that there is nothing to prove that humanity is anything other than mortal, this 'enfurecimiento', this going out of one's Self in order to contemplate divinity, takes place in a state of anguish, of radical doubt. It is an act of affirmation, an opening of the Self to the divine: 'Para el pensamiento cristiano, este anonadamiento enfurecido es la afirmación de una vanidad, de un vacío que abre, ansiosamente, nuestro ser humano al divino' (p. 43). But in addition it is an opening of the Self to the anguish of doubt, the attempt to maintain a belief in transcendence whilst accepting the annihilating implications of this act for the Self:

Y la furia trágica se hace trance angustioso, tránsito de agonía, dramática ansiedad. ¿Se hace entusiasmo, endiosamiento? ¿Jubilosa, espiritual alegría? ¿Entrar, enterarse de la nada, es, para el pensamiento cristiano, adentrarse en todo, enterarse de Dios? (p. 43)

The questioning nature of this stance is underlined by Bergamín. The figuring of the quest for transcendence implies that one exists in this world in a state of estrangement, estrangement from God. One's existence appears partial, a shadow of a greater possibility:

La dialéctica de la voluntad y el deseo, de la angustia y de la ansiedad, del ser y de la nada, proyecta a este ser humano en el mundo, por su mismo tiempo pasajero, como la silueta quijotesca, la oscura sombra gesticulante que decíamos, sobre un cielo cerrado como sobre un muro, de la llama viva. (p. 43)

For Bergamín, true Christian personhood requires the repeated denial of the structures of identity as they exist in the material world, a continual refocusing upon the divine, and the containment of a paradox. The material Self must be accepted as illusory: the search for true personhood demands the painful consciousness of the illusory nature of Self. This consciousness along with the urge to overcome the stricture of death informs Bergamín's vision of the dialectics of faith as a dialectic which depends for its vital spark upon the notion of anguish, agony, passion, or radical doubt:

Se encuentra el ser en ese mundo por perderse en él, como Don Quijote; enajenado, por su pasión, de la misma razón que lo determina, que lo expresa y define en el tiempo o por el tiempo de ese modo. *Este laberinto de su enajenación racional ¿no es en el hombre el ámbito que forma y decide su pensamiento? ¿No es su lógica viva? ¿La dialéctica de su pasión humana?* (p. 43, my italics)

The state of anguish provoked by the faith/doubt dialectic, though apparently a negative state of suffering, paradoxically foments Bergamín's only possibility of apprehending the divine:

En este laberinto de espejos en que se verifica el ser por el ámbito de su nada, que le rodea como de un purgatorio ardiendo de invisibles llamas, se espeja o refleja en múltiples imágenes, infinitamente, aquella semejanza divina por la que se pierde y se encuentra el hombre como un fantasma o sombra perseguida y perseguidora de sí misma. (p. 43)

It is evident, then, that Bergamín's notion of personhood is shaped by his attitude towards faith as the prime mover in his thought. Just as the act of going out of oneself is a passionate act, an 'enfurecimiento' which opens man to the divine, so too, for Bergamín, is art a process of life-renewal which makes an appeal to the divine. The poetic act is in essence a religious act. He says of art, or more precisely of poetic thought:

La razón de ser de todas las artes poeticas es este pensamiento recién nacido de la razón divina: este pensamiento puro; y por eso son nuevas las artes: porque son poéticas, porque acaban, siempre, herméticamente, de nacer. Y son nuevas, cuando lo son, porque son, sencillamente, antediluvianas.[9]

Thus poetic discourse, because it is according to Bergamín a privileged discourse, has the divine potential of the eternally original and new. Ideally, therefore, the artist releases a divine vision.

By extension, for Bergamín a religious approach to life is essentially artistic because such an approach seeks to reveal 'la razón divina'. Life and art are enmeshed in the agony of religious being, a process of continual rereading. Life and art are activities in common. Both are defined as parts of a religious sensibility, a conceptual conflation which Bergamín justifies in an etymological way:

Releer, en suma. En el *Libro de las Etimologías*, de San Isidoro de Sevilla [...], leemos que el santo se inclina a darle al término 'religioso' el sentido etimológico que le dio Cicerón de 'a relegando'. Nos dice el etimologista primitivo: 'Religiosus, de "a relegando", el que lee muchas veces, el que relee: 'Leyendo muchas veces - dice - porque lee las cosas que pertenecen al servicio y honra de Dios.' Lee, relee libros sagrados, escrituras santas.[10]

Reading is a descriptive and affirmative act and to this extent writing and reading are indistinguishable from each other. Both reading and writing are repetitive in nature, rereading and rewriting. Writing persists through rereading: 'Un libro es duradero, perdurable, por la capacidad de relectura inacabable que nos ofrece por su incitación religiosa. En una palabra, por su espíritu' (p. 86). A religious person is one who continually rereads: 'Y el que lee y relee de ese modo es hombre de relectura, esto es, de religión, es hombre religioso' (p. 84), and the religious act is a continuous act of realignment towards transcendence. The religious imperative for Bergamín is one of connection, self-knowledge through connection, the tidal process of continual renewal:

Pues el que lee se liga a sí mismo en lo que lee, para, releyéndolo, religarse — religiosamente — con ese propósito o voluntad, santísima voluntad humana, de un puro saber que no quiere olvidarse por tan puramente saberse. Saberse a sí mismo: saborearse. (p. 84)

So, art and life are not only activities in common, art is also an investment in the feeling of being alive:

La literatura no se aprende, se sabe, como todo lo que se sabe, primero se sabe y después se aprende. La literatura se aprende de ese modo vivo; se prende o aprehende, partiendo vivamente de su sabor o sabrosa sabiduría propia. [...] La literatura es leer y escribir de veras, vivamente. Y escribir y leer es hablar: es lo que se habla, se imagina, se fabulea, se hace fabuloso; se vuelve lenguaje verdadero y vivo: en una palabra, poesía: creación. Por eso hay que leer y releer para recrear — y recrearnos — con lo creado. Y escribir, como leer, es *hablar*; y hablar es *decir*; y decir es *pensar*; y pensar es *sentir*; y sentir es *sentirse vivo*.[11]

The dynamic process of the re-creation of the Self, the continual realignment of the Self within the labyrinth of one's estrangement from God signifies an active re-creation of one's consciousness of being alive through the re-creative processes of literature. This view of poetics, like Miguel de Unamuno's point of departure for *Del sentimiento trágico de la vida en los hombres y en los pueblos* (1913), elevates the sentimental and experiential spheres of human existence over that of rational truth. Bergamín sees the artist as a mythmaker who describes the experience of being alive in terms of the desire to remain alive and he sees poetics as a discourse which sets out to challenge the rational truth of material and mortal human existence.

CHRISTIAN POETICS

Bergamín's identification with the figure of Christ is sited in the realm of poetics, and he feels that only poetic discourse is adequate to the task of comprehending the dynamism of Christian symbolism. Christianity yearns for the merging of the human and the divine. For Bergamín, it is only poetic discourse that can provide a crucial emphasis upon a dynamic dialectic of re-creation. The figure of Christ invokes and actualizes the agony of renewal, a primal state of coming into being, of rebirth symbolized for Bergamín in the image of the sea. Christ is crucified facing the sea and this image speaks of the agony of being alive and the intimacy of the Self, of personhood. Bergamín's 'Tres sonetos a Cristo crucificado ante el mar'[12] encapsulate the agony of being alive, the struggle, ('lucha'), or dialectics of faith, which shapes Bergamín's Christianity.[13] Bergamín understands, as Unamuno points out in *La agonía del cristianismo*, that the immortality of the body is as important as the immortality of the soul. According to Unamuno:

No sólo el alma, sino el cuerpo humano, el cuerpo que debe resucitar, quiere crear al Verbo, a fin de que éste cree el alma y la eternice, y al cuerpo, cuna y sepulcro del alma, al cuerpo donde el alma nace y desnace, muere y desmuere. Desnacer es morir y desmorir es nacer. Y esto es una dialéctica de agonía. (pp. 32-33)

The uneasy relationship between the intangibility of the soul and the materiality of the body comprises the marriage of opposites which propels the dialectics of faith for Bergamín on both a literal and a figurative level. Indeed, metaphor for Bergamín has bodily potential. He can only substantiate the divine nature of his poetics within a Christian context: it is not sufficient simply to ascribe to poetic language a purely spiritual or Hellenistic access to the divine. The poetic resolution of immortality is, as with the identification with Christ in the three sonnets below, both bodily and spiritual.

The trinity of sonnets to which I have been referring will become a touchstone of this study and so I cite them here in full:

Tres sonetos a Cristo crucificado ante el mar
(París, 1937)
A Jacques y Raïssa Maritain

Solo, a lo lejos, el piadoso mar
Unamuno

I

No te entiendo, Señor, cuando te miro
frente al mar, ante el mar crucificado.
Solos el mar y tú. Tú en cruz anclado,
dando a la mar el último suspiro.

No sé si entiendo lo que más admiro:
que cante el mar estando Dios callado;
que brote el agua, muda, a su costado,
tras el morir, de herida sin respiro.

O el mar o tú me engañan, al mirarte
entre dos soledades, a la espera
de un mar de sed, que es sed de mar perdido.

¿Me engañas tú o el mar, al contemplarte
ancla celeste en tierra marinera,
mortal memoria ante inmortal olvido?

II

Ven ya, madre de monstruos y quimeras,
paridora de música radiante:
ven a cantarle al Hombre agonizante
tus mágicas palabras verdaderas.

Rompe a sus pies tus olas altaneras
deshechas en murmullo suspirante.
De la nube sin agua, al desbordante
trueno de voz, enciende tus banderas.

Relampaguea, de tormentas suma,
la faz divinamente atormentada
del Hijo a tus entrañas evadido.

Pulsa la cruz con dedos de tu espuma.
Y mece por el sueño acariciada,
la muerte de tu Dios recién nacido.

III

No se mueven de Dios para anegarte
las aguas por sus manos esparcidas;
ni se hace lengua el mar en tus heridas
lamiéndolas de sal para callarte.

Llega hasta ti la mar, a suplicarte,
madre de madres por tu afán transidas,
que ancles en tus entrañas doloridas
la misteriosa voz con que engendrarte.

No hagas tu cruz espada en carne muerta;
mástil en tierra y sequedad hundido;
árbol en cielo y nubes arraigado.

Madre tuya es la mar: sola, desierta.
Mírala tú que callas, tú caído.
Y entrégale tu grito arrebatado.

(*Poesías casi completas*, pp. 23-24)

The cycle of poems documents the process of mythical renewal as it is revealed to the poet, who struggles to understand the relationship between eternal life and oblivion and, in turn, the functioning of that dialectic in the 'mortal memoria' of the 'Hombre agonizante', the construction of infinity in the finite world of man's identity. What is striking is the muteness of the mortal wound in the side of Christ when, in contrast, the sea can never really be silent: it is always a residual babble, 'murmullo suspirante', mythically, magically preparing to give birth to eternal life, the godchild, 'Dios recién nacido'. A feminine principle is the instigator of the divine, the supremely generous sea receives and transforms and atones, 'at-ones' for the agony of man:

> Llega hasta ti la mar, a suplicarte,
> madre de madres por tu afán transidas,
> que ancles en tus entrañas doloridas
> la misteriosa voz con que engendrarte. [...]
>
> Madre tuya es la mar: sola, desierta.
> Mírala tú que callas, tú caído.
> Y entrégale tu grito arrebatado.

The coming into divinity constitutes the acquisition of voice, a voice which is, paradoxically, a voice that is at once indivisible without being individual, an at-oneness with the sea which is 'sola' and 'desierta'.

I shall return to these sonnets in due course. However, for the moment I wish to signal the relevance of this yearning for a personhood without individuality which informs Bergamín's concept of Self as a notion that is apparently always negativized in his writing:

> No soy ahora ni aquí.
> No tengo tiempo ni sitio.
> No me quedo ni me voy.
> No estoy sin ti ni contigo.
> No tengo nunca ni siempre.
> No soy el fin ni el principio.
> No te encuentro ni te busco.
> No te huyo ni te sigo.
> No, no, no, no, no, no ,no...
> No será lo que no ha sido.
> - Pues dime, ¿quién eres tú
> si no eres otro ni el mismo?
> - Soy lo que no tiene nombre:
> lo que no tiene sentido.
> - Ahora sí que te conozco:
> eres mi mejor amigo.
>
> (*Poesías casi completas*, p. 74)

Selfhood is imagistically portrayed as a lack, a questioning space in his poetry and yet critics such as Nigel Dennis refer to Bergamín as continually present in his work. Given Bergamín's vision of selfhood, Dennis's reading of the poet's poetic voice of oblivion can be seen as a misreading. He states:

Cada libro es, ante todo, diría yo, una versión en miniatura de ese laberíntico artefacto total que constituye la expresión completa del pensamiento del escritor. En este sentido puede afirmarse que Bergamín, como otros escritores de muchos quilates, *está totalmente presente en casi cada línea que escribe.*[14]

Here Dennis claims to be talking about the personality of Bergamín. However, given that Bergamín casts himself as barely existent, such a personality is, paradoxically, defined through its lack of definition, its lack of individuality, though it may well be that the statement of such is impressive and indelible since it inscribes Bergamín's doubtful subjectivity. This much Luis Suñén accredits to Bergamín's voice when he comments on his *La importancia del demonio (y otras cosas sin importancia):*[15]

Recordaría ahora — y conviene no olvidarlo en la lectura que nos ocupa — sus palabras en ese extraordinario soneto a Rafael Alberti: '... perdiendo con su sueño nuestra vida'. Se refiere Bergamín en sus palabras a seguir '... los pasos peregrinos de una patria perdida'. Y debe quedar claro eso. Bergamín sabe a cada momento en qué lugar se mueve y desde dónde lanza su palabra. Y su palabra parte de la vecindad del lugar analizado. *Nunca se olvida Bergamín de sí mismo en el análisis de una realidad más o menos cercana, a la que su presencia no puede sustraerse.* Y de esta cercanía, de este roce, de esta fusión en ocasiones, no puede sino salir esa crítica creadora que Bergamín nos ofrece a través de su original indagación.[16]

Herein lies the confusion surrounding the figure of Bergamín. The poet writes about personality, but he locates personality beyond the Self and in particular beyond himself. The rhetorical figure he uses to allude to his existential dilemma is confusing to critics who insist on seeing Bergamín as an 'hombre importante'. Bergamín is not talking about *who* he is so much as *whether* he is and, *if* he is, where and how he is being. Life's dilemmas are in this sense personal dilemmas which have much in common with the 'personnaliste' doctrines of the *Esprit* movement.[17] The question of personhood for Bergamín has to be seen in the context of twentieth-century Christianity. If the critic is blind to this then Bergamín the person is liable to take precedence over the Bergamín who describes what it is to be a person.

Nigel Dennis and Luis Suñén are, however, gesturing towards the stylistic features of Bergamín's writings as characteristic of his poetic voice. Indeed, the use of paradox, etymological reasoning, and a certain hermeticism so easily associated with Bergamín are also characteristic of his religious attitude in that his subject matter appears to foment such stylistic acrobatics. In this sense stylistic hermeticism can be seen as a feature of Christian Existentialism. Bergamín himself was aware on the one hand, for instance, of the inadequacy of language to speak of God:

> Poeta, tu razón de ser
> no es ser de razón engendro;
> Dios no inventó un diccionario
> cuando creó el universo;
> ni para nombrar las cosas
> utilizó un alfabeto;
> ni consultó la gramática
> cuando empezó el Verbo.

(Poesías casi completas, p. 74)

Equally, though, he sensed the reluctance of man to make language yield its full potential. Bergamín reasoned etymologically and paradoxically. He used mystical and mysterious, mystifying terminology in an attempt to exploit the magical, otherly potentials of his poetic language. I shall be considering the place of such a discourse further on in this study, though I simply wish to point out at this stage that the subject matter of Bergamín's work demands a certain hermeticism because he considers that he is struggling on the edges of language and, literally for him, on the edges of mortality, of life:

Trazando la naturaleza y figuración fronteriza de la poesía, encontramos, en sus fronteras, una sola letra inicial por las que todas sus definiciones nominales comienzan: letra inicial que es la de la muerte.[18]

Like personhood, poetry folds in upon itself in order, paradoxically, to surpass its own deathly limits:

Cuando la poesía vuelve sobre sí misma su propio sentir y sentido, cuando *se ensimisma*, se concentra, definiéndose, delimitándose, trazando sus fronteras, por su propia magia o metafísica, mística, moral y música, que la encierra en círculos concéntricos definidores de ese ensimismamiento, como cuando se enfurece y halla fuera de sí aquel mismo sentir y sentido que buscaba dentro, la poesía se pregunta por la muerte. Dentro o fuera del hombre, esa es la línea definidora de la poesía. (p. 9)

Poetic language in this scheme of things promises new potential, new semantic elasticity directly related to the acquisition of a vision of eternity or of the eternally new. If this language is fully exploited by the poet, poetry can become the vehicle of salvation:

Desde Dante hasta Nerval, la poesía traza su línea definidora en ese principio espiritual de una *vida nueva* que afirma un más acá y un más allá de la muerte. La poesía tiende a afirmar su figuración o ficción imaginativa por la voluntad de traspasar esa frontera definidora del ser vivo en el hombre. (p. 9)

PERSONNALISME

As I have been pointing out, one of the flaws in the critical appreciation of Bergamín to date has involved a failure to give credence to Bergamín's religious orientation. This, coupled with the stylistic difficulty of much of his work, has led to incomprehension and neglect. It is important to note, therefore, that Bergamín was not alone in his preoccupation with the place of religious sensibility in the modern age and the necessity of accommodating it to the nineteenth-century fin-de-siècle revolution of the notion of identity. The new pre-eminence of subjective discourse was also being answered by other religious writers such as Nicolas Berdyaev. The esoteric style Bergamín uses is similar to that of the 'personnaliste' Berdyaev, whose notion of personality throws light on Bergamín's own articulations of personhood and its intimate connection with the notion of transcendence:

> But personality in man is evidence of this, that the world is not self-sufficient, that it can be overcome and surmounted. [...] But personality, man as a person, is not a child of the world, he is of another origin. And this it is that makes him a riddle. Personality is a break through, a breaking in upon this world; it is the introduction of something new. Personality is not nature, it does not belong to the objective hierarchy of nature, as a subordinate part of it. [...] Man is a personality not by nature but by spirit.[19]

For Berdyaev, personality, or personhood, as I have been saying with regard to Bergamín, is a spiritual value that gives account of the relationship between the human and the divine. In Berdyaev's theory, personality is 'the absolute existential centre' (p. 26). It is the spiritual strength of personality which resolves the apparent contradiction between the human and the divine:

> For personality, however, infinity opens out, it enters into infinity, and admits infinity into itself; in its self-revelation it is directed towards an infinite content. And at the same time personality presupposes form and limit; it does not mingle with its environment nor is it dissolved in the world around it. Personality is the universal in an individually unrepeatable form. It is a union of the universal-infinite and the individual-particular. It is in this apparent contradiction that personality exists. (p. 22)

The will of the personality is a religious act, an affirmation of the divine in man, and crucially in modern man, who has discovered the unconscious:

> Personality is not a biological or a psychological category, but an ethical and spiritual one. Personality cannot be identified with the soul. Personality has an elemental-unconscious

foundation. Man in his sub-conscious is submerged in the blustering ocean of elemental life and is but partially rationalized. (p. 25)

Berdyaev's theory is an attempt to replace and reaffirm the validity of a religious, Christian sensibility in a post-Freudian world, a world which has to cope with a new pre-eminence of human subjectivity and materialism. Most of all, Berdyaev is reascribing to the religious a concept of spirituality that challenges the forces of rationality: 'Personality is rational being, but it is not determined by reason and it cannot be defined by the vehicle of reason' (p. 24). Berdyaev, like Bergamín, describes a paradox. Personality operates for each outside the Self and yet the attainment of a 'personnaliste' stance involves intense subjectivization, 'ensimismamiento', an entering into subjectivity that consists of a vanishing into the Self, a transcendence of the Self which refuses objectivization. This process is a means of escape and at the same time an attainment of freedom. As can be seen in the following quotation, Berdyaev's description of the dynamic process of personality is rooted in the same conviction as Bergamín's — that of the essential estrangement of Man from God and the necessity to continually transcend the Self in order to escape the static, deathly trap of objectivization in favour of the repeated act of realignment of the finite self with the infinite divine:

The realization of personality in man is this continuous transcending of self. Man desires to go out from the closed circle of subjectivity and this movement always takes place in two different and even opposite directions. Emergence from subjectivity proceeds by way of objectivization. This is the way which leads out into society with its forms of universal obligation, it is the way of science with its laws of universal obligation. On this path there takes place the alienation of human nature, its ejection into the object world: personality does not find itself. The other path is emergence from subjectivity through the process of transcendence. This is a passing over into the trans-subjective and not to the objective. This path lies in the deeps of existence, on this path there take place the existential meeting with God, with other people, with the interior existence of the world. It is the path not of objective communication but of existential communion. Personality reaches full realization of itself only on this path. (p. 29)

I would not claim here that Bergamín is a Berdyaevian 'personnaliste', despite his frequent espousal of support for the *Esprit* movement.[20] However, there is obviously a certain affinity in their world views, especially with regard to the notion of personality as a paradoxical act of being where 'the spirit does not generalize but individualizes'.[21] Such poetic thinking and its stylistic peculiarity, concerning the containment of contradiction within the subject, is characteristic of both Bergamín and the 'personnalistes', whose joint concern is the description of the paradoxical nature of personality: 'It is a union of the universal-infinite and the individual-particular. It is in this apparent contradiction that personality exists.'[22] Consequently, I shall be investigating how Bergamín's Christian Existentialism informs his questioning stance towards the cultural hegemony of Reason, the discourse of certainty. His writings enact his faith, a faith which demands a reassessment of the fixed, and to him deathly, stillness of current Christian symbology. In his questioning stance towards Reason he aligns himself, from a deeply Hispanic perspective, with the religious tradition which feeds on the thought of anti-rationalists such as Pascal, Kierkegaard, Nietzsche, and Unamuno.

Although Bergamín's popularity in France has largely been due to his involvement in the theological debate around *Esprit* and Catholic Marxism, and also modern Christian Existentialism as espoused by Berdyaev, some stress needs to be laid on the wide-ranging cultural reference of Bergamín's work, which spans the literary canon of western culture as a whole and yet displays specifically Hispanic characteristics. For the poet, Christian concerns are Hispanic concerns and as such are played out through literary characters such as Cervantes's Don Quijote and Calderón's Segismundo.

To do justice to Bergamín one must not align him definitively with any contemporary group, because he did not concern himself with such temporary definition. Indeed, much of his work constitutes a refusal to be placed within historical time. José Luis Cano cites Bergamín himself when trying to resolve the difficulty of placing his work in a specifically historical context, suggesting that Bergamín's task is to deliberately place himself beyond the purely historical, to live out of time:

¿Es Bergamín un poeta que entrega su mensaje 'a contratiempo', como se definía Unamuno en el primer poema -'¡Id con Dios!'- de su primer libro de poesía? [...] A estas preguntas quizá conteste un poemita del propio Bergamín:

> Ahora al leerme estáis tal vez pensando
> que no soy de mi tiempo.
> Del mío sí. Pero tal vez ahora
> ya no lo soy del vuestro.
>
> El vuestro precipita el torbellino
> en que lo estáis perdiendo.
> El mío es un remanso sosegado
> lo mismo que un espejo.
>
> En estas soledades en que vivo
> me miráis como a un muerto:
> sin ver que es otra vida y otro mundo
> lo que llevo dentro.[23]

Of course the placing of Bergamín's work in a historical time is an integral part of this study and has been the specific task of other studies. These other studies, however, consistently refuse to acknowledge Bergamín's own attitude which, though consistent with his Christian outlook, grates on the nerves of the most persistent literary critics, whose hidden agenda, as I pointed out earlier, is always one of ejection from or inclusion into their own particular school of thought. My contention here is that, although it helps the reader to understand the historical context in which Bergamín writes, Bergamín's world view is one which he considers to be timeless. Thus to label Bergamín's work at all, let alone to label it as anachronistic, is to judge Bergamín's writing by criteria which he would consider to be hopelessly partial. It is not that Bergamín remains aloof from the workings of history, not at all, but that as the *Esprit* movement contended, and Bergamín echoed in his article 'Un gran vuelo de cuervos mancha el azul celeste': '*Hay valores espirituales que están por encima de toda política.*'[24]

CRITICAL 'PARTIDISMO'

The relationship between history and eternal time in Bergamín's world view becomes particularly complex when Bergamín's political profile is considered. His political argumentation is marked by a refusal to relinquish his poetic approach to both the style and content of his discourse. He favours eternal ideals over pragmatism. Again, this is due to the religious orientation of such a world view. Thus Bergamín's involvement in politics never ceases to answer his religious imperative to base his life upon the search for eternal values rather than upon the transient (and in his eyes infinitely corruptible) values of the material world.

One of the most resounding examples of his unbending commitment to eternal values can be seen in the way he criticizes the Spanish Church on the grounds of its inability to maintain purist eternal values. As an essentialist, Bergamín rarely defends what he considers to be unassailable ideals; he simply states what he sees as eternal values or truths, and so consequently his polemical writings take on a highly corrosive, critical tone, as will be apparent in the following analysis. Catholicism during the Second Republic and the Civil War in Spain became a controversial issue due to the repressive, conservative reputation of its official organ, the Church. In an article published in *Hora de España* in 1937, Bergamín sought to dissociate himself from a politically contaminated Church:

Constantemente, durante años, vine intentando, con mi pluma, por la palabra, romper esa monstruosa insensibilidad religiosa española que había encontrado su caparazón protector en la apariencia y tramoya de una Iglesia que ofrecía, al amparo de la descomposición del Estado, su propia estructura administrativa como caparazón en que ampararla, a su vez en mutuo auxilio, inmoral convivencia, entrelazándola en su corrupción misma.[25]

Bergamín repeatedly voiced his protest in a hysterical and polemical fashion, especially in the aftermath of the July 1936 insurrection. His protest is against the use of the Church for political ends, a protest which does not contradict the notion that all good Catholics should be politically responsible. First, he declares that, despite their protestations to the contrary, the representatives of the Church were indeed directly implicated in the outbreak of the Civil War:

La participación política de los sedicentes católicos, con la mayoría de los sacerdotes, religiosos y altas jerarquías eclesiásticas, en la sublevación militar de julio, único origen de nuestra actual situación dramática, de nuestra terrible lucha presente, no es una participación que pueda incluirse dentro de un proceso jurídico con actas notariales y otras demostraciones, literales o formales, del mismo tipo probatorio. No. Esta participación, que va desde la complicidad al encubrimiento, no puede encerrarse en los límites artificiosos de un amoldamiento jurídico. Es muy otra cosa. Es una participación viva, verdaderamente directa, en un proceso histórico, del cual esta revolución y guerra civil del presente no es más, como le digo, que la más dolorosa, espantosa, consecuencia. (Santonja, p. 81)

Then Bergamín goes on to unveil the discrepancy between the Church's avowed non-participation and the Christianization of the right-wing political agenda, an appropriation which he considers to be nothing short of sacrilegious:

Recuerde que la CEDA se decía representante de los católicos en España. [...] Tan naturalmente como sobrenaturalmente, para mí, el catolicismo no es eso; no puede, sin profanación, sin sacrílega impostura, admitirse siquiera su vinculación a nada de eso; como a ninguna otra, aunque fuese noble y digna, política determinada. Todos los textos más autorizados se oponen a esto. (Santonja, p. 82)

Bergamín salvages religion from the wreckage of the institution of the Church being used for political ends by singling out as personally culpable members of the clergy, such as the Bishop of Barcelona, who played an active part in Christianizing right-wing political attitudes: 'Este Obispo fue quien, en las elecciones de febrero último, predicó la cruzada contra el Frente Popular, identificando el votar a las derechas con el votar a Cristo' (Santonja, p. 83). In this open letter Bergamín's argument exemplifies a typical thought paradigm. He sets up a historical truth against an unassailable ideal. In this case, the Christian ideal is being falsely claimed by the representatives of the Church and used in the interests of the political right wing. Bergamín argues that the Church's representatives are demeaning Christianity:

Son dos cosas muy diferentes, a mi juicio, las que usted, Monsieur Gay, parece involuntariamente confundir. La posición, por así decirlo, oficial, de la Iglesia española, esto es, de sus altas jerarquías dirigentes al advenimiento de la República, y la conducta de estos mismos dirigentes desmintiendo constantemente aquella posición de principio. (Santonja, p. 83)

He, in turn, takes up the banner of eternal ideals and insists that only a revolutionary stance can protect the eternal ideals of Christianity. Having set up this comparison, Bergamín argues passionately for his stance saying that he would prefer to have no Church at all than one which is contaminated with a hypocrisy which is fostered by the inappropriate involvement of the Church in current historical events. Thus, he claims for himself an idealistic integrity which he has wrested from his adversaries in the Church:

Pues, yo le digo, Monsieur Gay, que prefiero que en algún tiempo no haya culto público religioso alguno en mi país, que no el que éste se profane en tales extremos sacrílegos; que a eso lleguen los Obispos facciosos, traicionando su fe como su patria; hasta bendecir las máquinas de guerra, las terribles armas de muerte con que se asesina a nuestro pueblo. (Santonja, p. 87)

Bergamín's attitude is of course the attitude of a revolutionary rather than that of a reformer. He rejected the notion of reform as a principle which he considered to be profoundly uncreative, even anti-creative. For Bergamín, that which is not positively creative is not only passive but actually destructive. There could be no half-measures, as is indicated in the following aphorisms from *El cohete y la estrella*:

La palabra Reforma, con mayúscula o con minúscula, es una palabra antipática.
Reformación, renovación, reconstrucción: impotencia para destruir y para formar y construir de nuevo.
Reformador es el que no sabe hacer ni deshacer.
La reforma no es lo que forma, sino lo que deforma.
Si reforma es deformación, transformación es escamoteo de la forma.
Lo más parecido a un reformador es un transformista.[26]

Bergamín attributes nastiness to the very word 'Reforma' and gives his allegiance, after Malraux, to the process of revolution as an artistic, creative act of coming into consciousness:

André Malraux, este escritor amigo que unió con tanta fuerza su destino al nuestro, nos decía: 'El destino total del arte, el destino total de todo lo que los hombres expresan en la palabra cultura, está contenido en una sola idea: transformar el destino en conciencia. Por eso el destino, en sus varias formas, debe ser primero concebido, para poder ser luego dominado.' De día en día, de pensamiento en pensamiento, los hombres rehacen el mundo a imagen de su más elevado destino. La Revolución les da sólo la *posibilidad* de su dignidad; y cada uno de ellos ha de transformar esa posibilidad en una posesión. En cuanto a nosotros, intelectuales — cristianos, liberales, socialistas, comunistas —, a pesar de la ideología que nos divide, indaguemos un propósito común. Cualquier pensamiento sublime, cualquier obra de arte, pueden ser reencarnados en un millón de formas. Y nuestro antiguo mundo puede derivar su significado tan sólo de la voluntad actual del hombre.[27]

For Bergamín, the revolutionary sensibility is a universal principle based on the idea that personal consciousness should be a continuous, changing and creative act, a leap into the sublime, a testing, transforming, and reaffirming of truths. Bergamín recalls Larra in his insistence upon the sublime nature of revolution, describing the power of the imagination which, in its freedom to dream, in its ability to transform, and by its revolutionary nature, will seek out its 'destino fuerte',[28] its truth: 'Porque las pasiones en el hombre siempre serán verdades. Porque la imaginación misma, ¿qué es sino una verdad más hermosa?' (Santonja, p. 125). It is the imaginative freedom of Larra which fascinates Bergamín. Freedom and movement seek truth, hence truth must always be revolutionary, and always escaping constraint:

Hombres liberales, hombres libres — o liebres —, hombres peregrinos, pasearon su hastío entre claras lunáticas de ilusión. Porque de ilusiones se vive. Porque de ilusiones se vive cuando no se vive de verdad; cuando se vive de verdad, de ilusiones se muere. Las ideas más peregrinas, las más libres, o liberales, las ideas que corren sobre ellos, como sobre todas las cosas, no les alcanzarán. Los pasaron sin verles. Los pasaron de listos. Evoquemos por ellas al hombre libre o liebre, peregrino en su patria: Larra.[29]

The revolutionary as a universal principle informs every area of Bergamín's thought. It is essential to his conception of Christianity and indissoluble from it. Bearing this in mind, it is easy to see how Bergamín comes to suppose that the contamination of the Church is metaphysical in nature: the tyranny of history over eternal values, the constraints of the historical moment, and the corrupt, casuistic definitions of man in the pursuit of earthly power:

Ese falso catolicismo nacional, patrimonio de ricos, monopolio capitalista, es una corrupción visible de la verdadera Iglesia cristiana que traiciona, demoníaca, en el tiempo. Es peor que una mentira mortal; porque es una impostura que enmascara la verdad doblemente cuando con una mano entrega dinero para comprar armas al odio y con otra las bendice.[30]

It is precisely Bergamín's appeal to eternal values, and in particular to Christian values, which has alienated many of his political and literary critics. It is his appeal to transcendence, and his optimistic assumption that somewhere the ideal of transcendence exists uncontaminated by a worldly, self-servingly political message that disturbs the materialist thinkers of his time. Bergamín's stance has been caricatured in a new-versus-old dichotomy. Even now socialist critics find it hard to hide their scorn for the left-wing Catholic.[31] To them Bergamín is drawing connections where none exist or alternatively drawing distinction where there is no difference. For instance, he distinguishes between right-wing and left-wing Catholics and yet he fails to differentiate the realm of art from life. Bergamín's critics rail against his apparent conceptual vagueness concerning politics and religion, and even image and reality.[32] In his defence I contend that Bergamín intends to undermine the conceptual framework of the modern world, contesting on the one hand claims to a non-transcendent materialism in art and left-wing politics and, on the other hand, attacking uncritical attitudes to religious, political, and artistic values that parade as eternal when they are fuelled by a dominant phallocratic discourse of power. His problem though, as with his critics, is always and ever the problem of definition in language. So his main task is one of delving into language to awaken its forgotten potential. He adheres to the speaking of truths which, because they are religious, he shouts with religious zeal:

Que, como decía Santa Catalina, son estas las verdades que conviene decir a gritos. La tortura que por el fuego expresaron nuestras iglesias, puso estos gritos en el cielo. Clamaba al cielo expresamente esa llama purificadora. (Santonja, p. 85)

The initial hostility of Bergamín's contemporaries was both specific to the political climate in Spain during the Second Republic and also the product of a more general incapacity of the world to allow the unification of Catholic and Marxian ideals. It is interesting to note, however, that even in 1988 the problem of Bergamín's political affiliations still made left-wing, socialist critics wary of endorsing Bergamín's work wholeheartedly. For instance, the assumption that Bergamín's religious attitudes contaminate his political integrity colours Sabina de la Cruz's assessment of his career. Her dismissiveness of Bergamín is thinly disguised in her interview with Silvana Savini. Initially she lauds him as someone who represented left-wing Catholic thought. However, she only substantiates her praise by giving Bergamín credit for recognizing and bringing to the attention of the reading public the really great writers of the 'Generación del 27'. These were presumably the true 'juventud creadora' rather than Bergamín himself:

Su figura es primordial, representó un pensamiento católico, católico de izquierdas. Además, tuvo un papel muy importante como editor; él es uno también de los que edita a Federico García Lorca. O sea, que él, Altolaguirre, Prados, son los editores de los escritores que entonces, durante la guerra, eran la juventud creadora.[33]

Sabina de la Cruz, having damned with faint praise, clearly finds it difficult to square her dismissal of Bergamín with his lifelong political commitment to the Republic, which she admits, grudgingly, suggesting even that he was never one of the 'más avanzados ideológicamente'. (Savini, p. 16) Seemingly unaware of her own 'partidismo', Sabina de la Cruz deftly undermines her praise of Bergamín´s political integrity, her vision of the primordial nature of

3

his political importance, by situating such importance firmly within the pre-Civil War period. Furthermore, her praise of him as 'un personaje clave, importantísimo en la preguerra' (Savini, p. 16) is rendered still more provisional by her relegation of Bergamín's creative capacity to that of editorial skill:

Me parece que Bergamín, dentro del panorama literario y de la vida literaria, es un personaje clave, importantísimo en la preguerra. Pensemos en dos dimensiones: una como ideólogo de primera fila, el que representa todo un pensamiento católico y progresista: como creador es ya más discutible, sobre todo si se le intenta asociar de una manera valorativa a la 'Generación del 27'. En cualquier caso, dentro de la historia de la literatura es una figura de primera línea. Y como editor desarrolla una actividad de innegable valor. (Savini, p. 16)

When Sabina de la Cruz comes to her analysis of the post-Civil War period, again it is possible to detect a certain provisionality in the nature of her praise. Bergamín was exiled twice from Spain between the periods 1939-58 and 1963-70. The critic suggests that, when he was in Spain, Bergamín became a victim not only of the right but also of a mellowing left wing who no longer stood by their true Republican principles:

Y el auge económico dio posibilidades de vivir mejor, etc., crear editoriales, y se empiezan a 'desmarcar', diciendo que siguen siendo tan luchadores como siempre, pero eso conlleva que los 'puros' (los que bajo ningún concepto quieren comprometerse con la sociedad del régimen franquista) son eliminados, apartados y caídos en el ostracismo — y esto coincide con la crítica a la poesía social —. Yo creo que Bergamín es una de las víctimas de esta situación. Así, Bergamín recibe un doble golpe: por una parte lo recibe de las autoridades franquistas (por encabezar el manifiesto) y por otra parte lo recibe por la izquierda. (Savini, p. 17)[34]

Her mention of 'poesía social' tacitly acknowledges that in this era Bergamín is identifiable as politically heroic simply by association with Blas de Otero.[35] Nevertheless, I would dispute the portrayal of Bergamín as a victim. He may have been victimized, but the idea that he could not defend himself, at least 'por la palabra', is unacceptable to anyone who is acquainted with his combative and at times extremely provocative ways of reacting to his socio-political environment. Bergamín had suffered the consequences of the Civil War through his exile and there is no reason to suppose that he was unaware at any time of the effect his views would have on the Franquist régime: nor was he unaware of the instability of the left and the politics of convenience.[36] The idea that Bergamín was somehow incapable of matching the political needs of the day by refusing to accept the monarchy is to belittle his experience of political persecution, his political acumen, and his integrity.[37] He was, after all, rejected in the last years of his life not because of his anachronistic concern for the Civil War but rather for his outspoken views on the current political situation in Spain. It seems ridiculous that Sabina de la Cruz should portray the aging Bergamín as someone who merely sought refuge in his family by going to the Basque country: 'Por otra parte, ¿dónde encuentra Bergamín la acogida que necesitaba? Se refugia en su familia, que reside en el País Vasco' (Savini, p. 17). Only when Bergamín could no longer speak for himself was his name spoken in vain: his funeral was, admittedly, used for Basque separatist propaganda purposes. However, even in this instance Bergamín may not have been displeased. He had written in his last years of his concerns regarding Basque politics:

El entierro estuvo organizado por los 'abertzales' como un acto de propaganda. [...] A Bergamín se le ha apartado mucho, precisamente por su relación con los círculos 'abertzales' y creo que esto es injusto. (Savini, pp. 17-18)

It is unclear in this last statement of Sabina de la Cruz whether or not she is suggesting that Bergamín had been unjustly associated with the Basques or whether he had been unjustly rejected by the mainstream because of it. I have referred to Sabina de la Cruz at length because I believe that the type of confusion she expresses is exemplary of the critical anxiety that characterizes work on Bergamín. I also feel the need to defend his psychological coherence in his final years, since the main concern of this study is to evaluate Bergamín's poetic production, which he only published prolifically in the last two decades of his life. The writings of an old man may well be about death but need not be about, or reveal, senile decrepitude.

THE FRUSTRATION OF THE READER'S EXPECTATIONS

Sabina de la Cruz's circumspect analysis is not malicious or unconcerned, rather she suffers from the same difficulty that other critics experience when it comes to defining the significance of both Bergamín the person and Bergamín the writer. Bergamín thought of himself as principally a writer and even his political stance is consciously that of a writer.[38] Even in his 1979 electoral campaign he depicts himself as primarily a writer, albeit a Republican writer:

Y por este sabor del tiempo que os digo y porque el sargento Martín Villa ha prohibido ciertas palabras, y *yo soy hombre de palabras porque soy escritor*, me interesa citar algunas palabras, definiciones, no diré enteramente de mi tiempo, porque son del siglo XVI y XVII, pero casi, casi. Entre otras, la palabra Monarquía y la palabra democracia.[39]

And yet this self-definition clarifies little for those critics who hailed Bergamín as a creative writer. Again the 'personality' confusion arises and, most commonly, Bergamín is simply relegated to the rank of the unclassifiable:

Escritor versátil, que ha cultivado todos los géneros salvo la novela, José Bergamín quedará en la historia de la literatura española como un creador original, muy *sui generis*, inclasificable, agudo y lúcido como pocos, dotado de una lengua y estilo personalísimos.[40]

Indeed, José Luis Cano links Bergamín's personal style to the fact of the unclassifiable nature of his writings, though he explicitly acknowledges their creative and original character. Surprisingly, he simultaneously undermines his assertion by recognizing Bergamín's prestige in the critical rather than the creative field:

Pero Bergamín ha logrado más prestigio como ensayista que como poeta. Influido por el barroco español, por el conceptismo y por Unamuno, ha dejado escrita una extensa obra ensayística. (p. 5)

The personality cult surrounding Bergamín even at his death, instead of providing Bergamín with the recognition that Cano seeks for him, may actually diminish the stature in which he is held. One wonders, for instance, to what extent Bergamín's taste in young girls helps to focus the world's attention on his brilliance: 'Segundo exilio en París, donde se le solía ver en el café Flore, rodeado de amigos y de preciosas muchachas' (p. 5).

Similarly, Fernando Savater ascribes the notion of enigma to Bergamín, again talking specifically of Bergamín the person or personality, but significantly omitting the initial mention of his writings *per se*:

A fin de cuentas la paradoja de Bergamín, su fulminante contradicción, su íntima coherencia desconcertante y desconcertada, se expresan con una sola palabra, la que nunca comprenderá el dogmático ni el instrumentalista: enigma.[41]

Savater goes on to praise Bergamín's poetic production not as serious work but as play, as 'juego absoluto':

El pensamiento de las soledades es enigma, la poesía tiene su principio y su fin en la evidencia sola del enigma. No se aviene el enigma en su poética factura con lemas ni recetas; no funda una filosofía ni sirve para dirigir una política, sino que es lo más injurioso para el espíritu de seriedad: juego absoluto. Por eso no puede defenderse argumentalmente, ni explicarse, ni justificarse con las razones sin pasión ni magia que se emplean usualmente para aderezar el guiso de esas verdades que no son más que nuestros errores irrefutables, como advirtió el frecuentemente bergaminiano Gide. En cambio, el enigma no tiene significación, es signo absoluto, interrogación pura, sin respuesta, pero sin pregunta. (p.196)

This analysis is not so much erroneous as partial, a failure to concede the ludic quality in Bergamín's serious expression of a struggle between life and death. The tone of his poetry swings through despair, tranquillity, and mockery, his conceptual wordplay working as an integral part of his sketch of the emotions. His poetic voice is definitely ludic: however Fernando Savater fails to recognize the ludic qualities of Bergamín's style as an instrument of his expression, putting it forward, rather, as the raison d'être of his writing.[42] This stance, I would contend, undervalues Bergamín's fundamentally serious writerly intent.   Nevertheless, Fernando Savater, in passing, does reveal an intimate understanding of the conceptual traps that have dogged the critical appreciation of Bergamín's work. For instance, he points out that Bergamín is not a philosopher or a politician and that his arguments cannot be justified according to the rules of rationality. The critic proceeds to juxtapose Nietzsche and Bergamín:

Con los grandes enigmáticos — Nietzsche, Bergamín — se fabrican después mangas y capirotes los fúnebres ropavejeros del espíritu.   Y frecuentemente toman manga por hombro, risa por llanto, duda por fe, o los tres falsos enemigos del alma: mundo, demonio y carne por los tres auténticos: familia, municipio y sindicato. (p. 196)

It is important to note that Fernando Savater also considers Nietzsche to be an enigma and one assumes that he thinks of him as a poet, as Bergamín did, rather than as a great philosopher. Bergamín too describes Nietzsche as an enigma, but also as a poet and a prophet: 'misterioso enigmático, inquietante Nietzsche, el más oscuro poeta y tal vez más claro profeta de nuestro abismático tiempo.' (*Fronteras infernales de la poesía*, p. 196)

The possible and implied equation of Bergamín with philosophers makes the reader suspicious of critical claims concerning Bergamín's stature. Bergamín frequently writes about philosophers, refusing to treat any writer, including any philosopher, as anything other than a poet who describes what it is to be alive. The traditional myth of the philosopher as someone who is attempting to answer fundamental questions about what it is to be alive obfuscates the reader's perception of the poetic framework which Bergamín inhabits. First, he does not distinguish genre in general and, second, he situates himself in the realm of the poetic, in the world of the poets. For instance, the preface to *Fronteras infernales de la poesía* consists of a quotation from Nietzsche followed by its mirror-image, a paraphrasing in which Bergamín centres himself as companion and interlocutor of the poets he is about to give voice to:

En este libro encontrará el lector otras cuatro parejas inmortales y Nietzsche, Séneca, Dante, Rojas, Shakespeare, Cervantes, Quevedo, Sade, Byron, *fueron los ocho en que tuve puestos mis ojos, sintiendo en mí, como una sola sus miradas.* Cuatro parejas de sombras infernales que al darse y quitarse la razón entre sí, *al dármela o quitármela,* parecería que van acompañadas de Nietzsche, que acompañó su soledad con aquéllas otras. *También estas cuatro parejas infernales y Nietzsche acompañan la mía: las mías.* (p. 7, my italics)

Bergamín, who himself alludes to an equation of his own sensibility with those of the great thinkers of Western civilization aggravates the critical crisis of perspective that surrounds his work.[43]

It is necessary to separate two ways of thinking here: the vision the reader brings to the text of the function of the writer's models in his text and the way Bergamín actually thinks about other writers. What the reader expects to find disguises the content and intent of Bergamín's work. Again, this misapprehension, in the final instance, can be traced to a misunderstanding of the status of Bergamín's religious sensibility in his writings.

Obviously, to speak of reader expectation is a contentious area, fraught with theoretical and practical difficulties, not least of which is that of verifying any claims to be able to judge the true content of reader expectation and of the writer's intention. Nevertheless, one can gauge some basic suppositions as regards reader expectation simply by monitoring the nature of the critical accounts given of Bergamín's work. Writerly intent, too, is open to debate within the parameters of this study. This is simply because if one looks at Bergamín's work in the light of his religious sensibility his thought assumes a coherence which it lacks if a consideration of this area of his thought is not taken into account. The suggestion underlying this approach is that it is valid, critically speaking, to attempt an appraisal of a writer's work on the assumption that some coherent world view informs his poetic utterance. It is in this context that I suggest the following points for consideration concerning what I believe to be the misalignment of the critical approaches to Bergamín, such as those I have been discussing.

First, it can be assumed that one general underlying assumption brought to the critical appreciation of creative writing is the task of seeking to reveal the voice of the writer. Edward Saïd sees this as the signatory function of style:

Once again I must arbitrarily exclude all the more interesting complexities that go into making up the very question of style, in order to insist on style as, from the standpoint of producer and receiver, the recognizable and, repeatable, preservable sign of an author who reckons with an audience. Even if the audience is as restricted as his self or as wide as the whole world, the author's style is partially a phenomenon of repetition and reception. But what makes style receivable as the signature of its author's manner is a collection of features variously called idiolect, voice, or more firmly, irreducible personality.[44]

If Bergamín has a voice, it militates against the sort of singularity that Saïd describes above. If his voice is singular, it is singular because it speaks in tongues, usually other than his own. He describes his own voice as a lack of voice. It is this lack which is singular about his voice, this coupled with the ways he invites others, other writers, to speak for him. Bergamín implicitly accepts both the impersonality and transience of the text, filling his own with the more permanent voices of others, with multiple, otherly personalities and describing his own voice as continually escaping.

Bergamín's experience of the text is therefore similar to that described by Saïd: 'The paradox is that something as impersonal as a text, or a record, can nevertheless deliver an imprint or a trace of something as lively, immediate, and transitory as a "voice"' (p. 163). But Bergamín's reaction to this problem is wholly unexpected. Rather than echoing other voices, Bergamín sees himself as echoed in other voices. We shall come to understand this as one of the more positive features of the poet's experience of Self:

> Me estoy mirando en tus ojos.
> Me estoy oyendo en tu voz.
> Me estoy soñando en tu alma:
> sintiendo en tu corazón.
>
> Soy como si fuera otro:
> otro que quiere ser yo,
> y es un espectro, un fantasma,
> una sombra entre los dos.
>
> *(Poesías casi completas*, p.40)

We can say, then, that though Bergamín is aware of the paradoxical nature of the text, the form in which he wants to inscribe his voice or personality into it is not a straightforward affirmation of ego-identity. Modern theoretical notions about poetic voice seem to assume a univocity that is not evident in Bergamín's work, at least on the surface. So, for instance, Harold Bloom's work on the anxiety of influence is only partially applicable to Bergamín, simply because Bergamín does not subscribe to the notion that a poetic discourse is necessarily phallocratic in nature. If anything, Bergamín seeks to combat the propensity of language to engrain itself in a dominant patriarchal order. So, it is not necessarily problematic for Bergamín that poems, according to Bloom, are about '*other* poems':

Let me reduce my argument to the hopelessly simplistic; poems, I am saying, are neither about 'subjects', nor about 'themselves.' They are necessarily about *other poems*; a poem is a response to a poem, as a poet is a response to a poet, or a person to his parent. Trying to write a poem takes the poet back to the origins of what a poem *first was for him*, and so takes the poet back beyond the pleasure principle to the decisive initial encounter and response that began him. [...] *Only a poet challenges a poet as poet*, and so only a poet makes a poet. To the poet-in-a-poem, a poem is always *the other man*, the precursor, and so a poem is always a person, always the father of one's Second Birth.[45]

In fact, this return to the origin is precisely what Bergamín seeks and what is denied him by the static and unyielding and confusing nature of our worldy, demonic, misperceptions. Thus Bergamín says of Machado:

Para Antonio Machado, por boca de Mairena, el tiempo es cosa del Diablo; pero, si desapareciera, ni el Diablo, ni los poetas, existirían; porque no tendrían nada que hacer. Hacer tiempo, hacer memoria, que es hacer alma, ¿es el quehacer diabólico o divino de los poetas? Y ¿es hacer poesía? 'Porque ya, una cosa es la poesía y otra cosa lo que está grabado en el alma...' Y esa *otra cosa*, que, por la breve y precisa, honda y clara, misteriosa, luminosa obra poética y de pensamiento de Antonio Machado, se nos quedó grabada en el alma, ¿no es también poesía, la poesía?[46]

Here the return to the origin is a return to Poetry itself. Bergamín's appeal to transcendence, the humility of poetic creation in the face of an original and denied Poetry, an essence beyond the poet always, portrays the commonality of the poetic task. Bloom's 'misprision', for Bergamín, is itself a misinterpretation (*sic*): 'To live, the poet must *misinterpret* the father, by the crucial act of misprision, which is the re-writing of the father' (Bloom, p. 247).

To reduce the significance of writing within the literary canon to a consciousness only of itself, the writer's unconscious process of differentiation, the necessary though potentially annihilating nature of influence, denies the content of writing as if the commonality of human experience, Bloom's 'refusal of mortality', were irrelevant and uninteresting compared to the creation of personality, literary immortality. For Bergamín, the commonality of human expression interests him more than the univocity of his own expression. In fact this commonality depersonalizes the word as it focuses on the beyond. And this is one of the characteristics of Hispanic poetry: 'Y palabra española. Por eso ahonda su raíz en la tierra húmeda y levanta su ramaje en los cielos' (*De una España peregrina*, p. 202). Because what we continually misinterpret, what we continually miss, is an apprehension of the transcendent: we mistake the father for the origin. So Bloom asks who the father is, positing the idea that a writer has to resent, rebel against and even kill him to achieve his immortality:

But who, what is the poetic father? The voice of the other, of the *daimon*, is always speaking in one; the voice that cannot die because already it has survived death — *the dead poet lives in one*. In the last phase of strong poets, they attempt to join the undying *by living in the dead poets* who are already alive in them. This late Return of the Dead recalls us, as readers, to a recognition of the original motive for the catastrophe of poetic incarnation. Vico, who identified the origins of poetry with the impulse towards divination (to foretell, but also to become a god by foretelling), implicitly understood (as did Emerson, and Wordsworth) that a poem is written to escape dying. Literally, poems are refusals of mortality. Every poem therefore has two makers: the precursor, and the ephebe's rejected mortality. (Bloom, p. 247, Bloom's italics)

For Bergamín the 'refusal of mortality' is not only the common lot of poets but of humanity. This, of course is most clearly a legacy of Unamuno's point of departure in *Del sentimiento trágico de la vida en los hombres y en los pueblos*: 'Del único verdadero problema vital, del que más a las entrañas nos llega, del problema de nuestro destino individual y personal, de la inmortalidad del alma' (*Del sentimiento trágico de la vida*, p. 30). It is the voices of poetry which combat death: 'El poeta se pregunta a sí mismo por la muerte, y pregunta a sí mismo por la muerte, por su propio destino' (*Fronteras infernales de la poesía*, p. 9).

The significance for the individual of one's mortality is a problem in common that is not essentially related to the individuality of the writer, though the form, style or voice of his preoccupation with death provides the distinctive features of poetic voice, what Bergamín calls 'la retórica teatral del grito' (*Fronteras infernales de la poesía*, p. 13).

The notion of competition for immortality in literary terms is completely alien to Bergamín, for the poet writes about what it is to be alive and how to cope with death. The commonality of this content, accepted also by Harold Bloom, takes precedence over the individuality of its expression, the style of a writer only being valuable in so far as it speaks a language in common with other people. Life for Unamuno is an experience in common with all men whose defining feature consists in the effort not to die:

El esfuerzo con que cada cosa trata de perseverar en su ser no es sino la esencia actual de la cosa misma. Quiere decirse que tu esencia, lector, la mía, la del hombre Spinoza, la del hombre Butler, la del hombre Kant y la de cada hombre que sea hombre, no es sino el conato, el esfuerzo que pone en seguir siendo hombre, en no morir. (*Del sentimiento trágico de la vida*, p. 30)

Literary immortality is in this sense a false quest: to be remembered on earth is a poor reflection of a more insistent need to carry on living, not to die at all. This more insistent need is, according to Bergamín, only answered in Christ:

El hombre, para negarle a la muerte su morada, su guarida o manida, su cobijo, tendrá que negarse a sí mismo, paradójicamente, afirmándose con el signo trágico del hombre y el Dios, supliciado; afirmándose con aquello mismo que le niega: con la cruz. (*Fronteras infernales de la poesía*, p. 32)

Only in the context of a Christian sensibility is Bergamín able to refuse Harold Bloom's vision of the creative process, given that he functions as a poetic persona as-if-dead, as an 'esqueleto vivo, un fantasma perdido', a trope which contradicts Bloom's fundamental premise:

A poet, I argue in consequence, is not so much a man speaking to men as a man rebelling against being spoken by a dead man (the precursor) outrageously more alive then himself.

A poet dare not regard himself as being *late*, yet cannot accept a substitute for the first vision he reflectively judges to have been the precursor's also. (p. 247, Bloom's italics)

Evidently, critical work to date on Bergamín appears to be fraught with confusion. This confusion is stylistically at least a natural product of Bergamín's paradoxical mode of expression and historically it is partially accounted for by the partisanship of his contemporary and political commentators. More fundamentally, however, the religious and poetic orientation of his writing implicitly challenges some of the fundamental assumptions of the twentieth century and seems at times to render the reader blind to the subtlety of Bergamín's world view. His attempt to accommodate a vision of transcendence to a post-Nietzschean world in terms of a post-Freudian concept of identity, his rejection of materialism in favour of spirituality, his sidestepping of rational discourse in favour of a poetic language of desire all militate against Bergamín's historical acceptance and critical appreciation. Most significantly, the focusing of his gaze on a transcendent divine vision and his espousal of a dialectics of Faith in Christian terms, though acknowledged, has not been recognized as the prime mover of his thought and the force behind not only his religious writings but also his political as well as poetic production. Once the dialectics of Faith is viewed as essential not only to his religious thought but also to his sense of personhood and to his notion of creativity, the apparent quirkiness of many of Bergamín's views ceases to cause confusion and fits comfortably into the world view of an existentialist Christian whose preoccupation is not essentially with this life but with the next, not with the definition of individuality but with the possibility of overcoming subjectivity, not with the creation of literary immortality but with Christian immortality and of the elision of the material distinction between the finite and the infinite.

Many of the issues raised in this preliminary chapter will be examined in detail in the following chapters. The next chapter, in particular, is concerned with Bergamín's Christian poetics and his own creative literary criticism.

NOTES

[1] *José Bergamín*, ed. by Florence Delay and Dominique Letournier (Paris: Centre Pompidou, 1989).

[2] Antonio Garrigues Díaz-Cañabate, 'Les années *Cruz y Raya'*, trans. by Florence Delay, in Delay and Letournier, *José Bergamín*, pp. 71-75 (p. 75).

[3] Silvana Savini, 'Tres entrevistas sobre José Bergamín', *Rassegna Iberística*, 32 (September 1988), 9-18 (pp. 14-15).

[4] *Cruz y Raya: Revista de afirmación y negación*, ed. by José Bergamín (Madrid: Cruz y Raya, 1933-36).

[5] Nigel Dennis, *José Bergamín: A Critical Introduction, 1920-1936* (Toronto, Buffalo, and London: University of Toronto Press, 1986), p. 165.

[6] For an analysis of the gradual accommodation of Marxian ideas to Catholicism, especially with regard to the *Esprit* movement, see David Curtis, 'Marx against the Marxists: Catholic uses of the young Marx in the *Front Populaire* period (1934-1938)', *French Cultural Studies*, 2 (1991), 165-81.

[7] Giorgio Agamben, 'Du dandy au démonologue', in Delay and Letournier, *José Bergamín*, pp. 21-35 (p. 23).

[8] José Bergamín, *El pozo de la angustia*, 2nd edn (Barcelona: Anthropos, 1985), p. 42.

[9] José Bergamín, 'El pensamiento hermético de las artes', in *Cruz y Raya*, 15 April 1933, 41-66 (p. 45), my italics.

[10] José Bergamín, 'Leer y releer', in *Calderón y cierra España* (Barcelona: Planeta, 1979), pp. 83-87 (p. 84).

[11] José Bergamín as cited by Gonzalo Penalva Candela in his introduction to 'VIII. Temas varios' of José Bergamín, in *Antología periodística III*, ed. by Gonzalo Penalva Candela (Torremolinos: Litoral, 1984), pp. 45-47 (p. 45).

[12] José Bergamín, *Poesías casi completas*, 2nd edn (Madrid: Alianza,1984), pp. 23-24.

[13] See Unamuno's definition of 'agonía' as 'lucha' in Miguel de Unamuno, *La agonía del cristianismo*, 2nd edn (Madrid: Espasa Calpe, 1986), pp. 29-33.

[14] Nigel Dennis, *El aposento en el aire: Introducción a la poesía de José Bergamín* (Valencia: Pre-textos, 1983), p. 16, my italics.

[15] José Bergamín, *La importancia del demonio (y otras cosas sin importancia)* (Madrid: Júcar, 1974).

[16] Luis Suñén, 'La reflexión creadora de José Bergamín', *Cuadernos Hispanoamericanos*, no. 297 (March 1975), 681-84 (p. 682), my italics.

[17] José Bergamín knew many of the members of the French *Esprit* movement and publicized their work (through *Cruz y Raya*) in Spain. His theological stance has much in common with writers such as Emmanuel Mounier, Jacques Maritain, Nicolas Berdyaev as 'personnalistes', and Etienne Gilson as an existential Thomist. However, I would stress that Bergamín is not so much a theologian as a Christian creative writer and that it is a mistake to look for originality of theological thought in his work or to create artificial arenas for his work. To place him as an *Esprit* writer would be, for instance, to ignore the importance of other influences in his theological stance — in particular the relevance of the thought of the Protestant Christian existentialist, Paul Tillich, with regard to Bergamín's demonic perception of the material world. From a more immediate standpoint, one area in which Bergamín differentiates himself from writers such as Georges Bernanos in France is through his Hispanic outlook and his identification with figures of Hispanic literary discourse such as Cervantes's Don Quijote and Calderón's Segismundo. Incidentally, a study is yet to be done of Bergamín's influence on the *Esprit* movement's view, from France, of the Civil War in Spain, despite the availability of documentation of the lifelong spiritual and political debate between André Malraux and Bergamín. On this last point see, for instance, *André Malraux. Past, present and future: Conversations with Guy Suarès*, ed. by Guy Saurès, trans. by Derek Coltman (London: Thames and Hudson, 1974).

[18] José Bergamín, *Fronteras infernales de la poesía*, 2nd edn (Madrid: Taurus, 1980), p. 9.

[19] Nicolas Berdyaev, *Slavery and Freedom* (London: Bles, 1943), p. 21.

[20] See José Bergamín, 'Un gran vuelo de cuervos mancha el azul celeste', *Cruz y Raya* (March 1934), reprinted in *Cristal del tiempo 1933-1983*, ed. by Gonzalo Santonja (Madrid: Revolución, 1983), pp. 14-17. See also the proliferation of articles by members of the *Esprit* movement in *Cruz y Raya*, for instance Emmanuel Mounier, 'El movimiento y la revolución espiritual', (February 1934), reprinted in '*Cruz y Raya*': *Antología*, ed. by José Bergamín (Madrid: Turner, 1974), pp. 249-258, and Jacques Maritain, '¿Quién pone puertas al canto?', (April 1935), reprinted in '*Cruz y Raya*': *Antología*, pp. 295-316.

[21] Berdyaev, p. 29. In particular, Bergamín's emphasis on the body distinguishes him from Berdyaev.

[22] Berdyaev, p. 22.

[23] José Luis Cano, 'La poesía de José Bergamín', *Insula*, nos. 404-05 (July-August 1980), 16-17 (p. 16).

[24] José Bergamín, 'Un gran vuelo de cuervos mancha el azul celeste', *Cruz y Raya* (March 1934), reprinted in Santonja, *Cristal del tiempo*, pp. 14-17 (p. 16), Bergamín's italics.

[25] José Bergamín, 'Carta abierta a Madame Malaterre-Sellier, respondiendo al libro de Francisco Gay: "En las llamas y en la sangre"', (January 1937), reprinted in Santonja, *Cristal del tiempo*, pp. 79-89 (p. 84).

[26] Quoted in Santonja, p. 155.

[27] José Bergamín, 'Larra, peregrino en su patria, (1837 -1937) el antifaz, el espejo y el tiro', *Hora de España* (November 1937), reprinted in Santonja, pp. 111-26 (p. 126).

[28] I refer here to a recurring motif in Bergamín's work where he judges the message of poetic thought to be one of valour: 'Recordemos la lección clásica de nuestros poetas, que es como la de Shakespeare, como la de los griegos, la lección trágica del mundo: sólo un destino fuerte puede hacer fuerte nuestra libertad' (Santonja, pp. 125-26).

[29] Santonja, pp. 123-24.

[30] José Bergamín, 'Carta abierta a Madame Malaterre-Sellier, respondiendo al libro de Francisco Gay: "En las llamas y en la sangre"', *Hora de España* (January 1937), reprinted in Santonja, pp. 79-89 (p. 89).

[31] See Savini, pp. 15-16.

[32] See Dennis, *A Critical Introduction*, Chapter 6, pp. 136-80 (pp.146-52) for a detailed discussion of the critical reception of *Cruz y Raya*.

[33] Savini, pp. 15-16.

[34] The manifesto mentioned by Sabina de la Cruz refers to the 1963 'Carta-manifiesto dirigida al ministro Fraga Iribarne en protesta por la represión desencadenada contra los mineros asturianos' of which Bergamín was the first signatory. The letter caused his second banishment. See the letter of protest in Santonja, pp.151-54.

[35] It is interesting to note that Silvana Savini introduces Sabina de la Cruz first as Blas de Otero's partner and only subsequently as a university lecturer. Cruz raises no objection to this portrayal of herself as primarily a social appendage and only secondly as an autonomous intellectual. See Savini, p. 10.

[36] One has only to recall his public vilification in *España peregrina* of those who softened their left-wing political standpoint in the aftermath of the Civil War, and in particular his merciless attack on José Ortega y Gasset, to see how Bergamín had dealt previously with those who faltered in their political zeal. See José Bergamín, 'Españoles infra-rojos y ultra-violetas', *España peregrina* (February 1940), reprinted in Santonja, pp. 131-34, and also his 'Un caso concreto: contestado a don José Ortega y Gasset', *España peregrina* (February 1940), reprinted in Santonja, pp. 134-42.

[37] See Bergamín's articles on the transition to democracy and the reinstatement of the monarchy, in particular those he wrote in the period 1974-78 for the magazine *Sábado Gráfico,* which are reprinted in Santonja, pp. 155-212: 'Un mal paso' (January 1975), pp. 166-70; 'Viendo pasar la historia' (December 1975), pp. 174-79; 'Sueño y mentira de un Rey*'* (March-April 1978), pp. 200-04; 'Las ataduras' (April 1978), pp. 204-07; 'Reinar y Gobernar' (April 1978), pp. 207-12.

[38] It is in the role of a writer rather than as a politician that he signs the 'Carta-manifiesto dirigida al ministro Fraga Iribarne en protesta por la represión desencadenada contra los mineros asturianos', Santonja, pp. 151-54.

[39] José Bergamín, 'Hoy como ayer, mañana como hoy, España es republicana', Santonja, pp. 216-19 (p. 216), my italics.

[40] José Luis Cano, 'En la muerte de José Bergamín', *Insula*, no. 442 (September 1983), 5.

[41] Fernando Savater, 'Bergamín levanta el vuelo', in *Instrucciones para olvidar el 'Quijote' y otros ensayos generales* (Madrid: Taurus, 1985), pp. 195-97 (p. 196).

[42] Wordplay and punning are fascinating features of Bergamín's poetry. It is particularly interesting to look at his work in the light of Lacanian analyses of the pun for the bearing this has on the notion of identity crisis. See especially the following essays in *On Puns: The Foundation of Letters,* ed. by Jonathan Culler (Oxford: Routledge and Kegan Paul, 1988): Debra Fried, 'Rhyme Puns', pp. 83-99; Avital Ronell, *The Sujet Suppositaire*: Freud and Rat Man', pp. 115-39; Françoise Meltzer, 'Eat Your *Dasein*: Lacan's Self-Consuming Puns', pp. 156-63.

[43] *Fronteras infernales de la poesía* is an example of the spirit of 'compañerismo' in which Bergamín refers to, consumes, though rarely subsumes, other writers' words and ideas into his own texts as an integral part of a creative process which seeks a common voice, or more accurately, common voices with which to describe the condition of the human spirit. He glosses other writers in much the same way in his poetry. I would repeat that, to this extent, the last thing Bergamín desired was a sense of individuality which is, of course, why he confuses his critics.

[44] Edward W. Saïd, 'The Text, the World, the Critic', in *Textual Strategies: Perspectives in Post-Structural Criticism,* ed. by Josué V. Harari (London: Methuen, 1980), pp. 161-88 (p. 163).

[45] Harold Bloom, 'Poetic origins and final phases', in *Modern Criticism and Theory,* ed. by David Lodge (London and New York: Longman, 1988), pp. 241-52 (p. 247), Bloom's italics.

[46] José Bergamín, 'Las telarañas del juicio — ¿Qué es poesía?', in José Bergamín, *De una España peregrina* (Madrid: Al-Borak, 1972), pp. 179-203 (p. 203).

CHAPTER 2

ART AND TEMPORALITY

THE POETIC FIGURING OF THE QUEST FOR IMMORTALITY

Bergamín's notion of art suffers the same misreading as does his literary persona. He considers all art to be a common quest for transcendence, so that great art is not a statement of individuality but a facing up to death. Genre in this sense is an irrelevance for Bergamín, although critical debate on his work has revolved largely around a need to attribute generic coherence to it. All art is poetic for Bergamín and all poetics face up to, challenge, death. Again, the justification for this is religious or to do with faith. Reason tells us we will die, whereas faith challenges death and seeks immortality. So, for Bergamín, poetry is anti-rational. He extrapolates this idea in *La estatua de don Tancredo*.[1] Don Tancredo pretends to be a statue in the bullring: he pretends to be immortal by creating himself as art. He goes out of himself and becomes other, and yet lives the fallacy of this; in this sense he lives the struggle/contradiction between faith and doubt, immortality and death. He also elides the difference between the poet and the poem. Don Tancredo distils the passion for immortality rather than creating an object of immortality. This distinction between the creation of something that is immortal and the poetic figuring of the quest for immortality is connected to what I call the Priapic Complex. The former, embodied in the image of the Eiffel Tower, is an example of the dominant male ego or the phallus, whereas the latter, for instance Don Tancredo, empowers the feminine, the powers that are beyond the human/masculine. Temporality is what Bergamín has to flee, and art as an immortal monument still implies temporality. Cursive time is a deathly, usually masculine time whereas eternal, monumental time partakes of the feminine and escapes temporality. This chapter seeks to show how Bergamín's attitude to poetics is informed by a religious need to challenge the temporal restrictions of human existence, restrictions which he considers to have been dangerously belittled in the modern age because of man's delusions of grandeur and his lack of concern for the way in which phallocratic rational discourse denigrates otherness, which falls into the symbolic category of the feminine.

The notion of transcendence, with its attendant manifestation as the feminine divine, implies a rejection of definition because it claims to inhabit a realm which lies beyond conceptualization. Paradoxically, therefore, the substance of Bergamín's work tends to undermine the work of his critical commentators whose task is that of definition within a historical framework.

Don Tancredo's attempt to escape the strictures of human time and identity in favour of immortality through art exemplifies an attitude to art which has been consistently overlooked by Bergamín's commentators, concerned as they are with defining his work within a literary tradition. Such definition has become a particularly thorny issue against a European cultural background which in the first decades of the twentieth century thrived on the notion of vanguard movements and the '-ism' fetish. Usually, critical debate about Bergamín revolves both around the notion of genre and around the status of the place conceded to him in the 'Generación del 27'. The critical approach to Bergamín's work is complicated by his own vision of the place and function of art, for him 'las artes poéticas'. Once again, both Bergamín's vision of art and the critical debate about his place in the canon is affected, shaped, and critically clarified by a consideration of his religious sensibility.

The critical debate around the notion of genre and Bergamín's place in the 'Generación del 27' often appears confused and is essentially misleading, focusing as it does, inappropriately for him, upon definitions of art and temporality which prove to be anathema to Bergamín himself. For instance, in the following analysis, the commonplace distinction between prose and poetry proves insufficient and obfuscatory. Francisco C. Lacosta, for example, confirms the typical definition of Bergamín as predominantly an essayist and literary critic: 'Se puede decir que es ante todo un ensayista y un crítico de amplia formación literaria y filosófica.'[2]

Certainly, most of Bergamín's published writing before the 1960s consisted of literary criticism, political, often polemical articles, theological essays, and writings concerned with the Hispanic sensibility. He also published several collections of aphorisms, some plays, and a handful of poems including a few political satires.[3] The main body of his poetry was only published during the last two decades of his life and posthumously, although it was seemingly common knowledge that Bergamín wrote poetry, almost daily, in the form of a 'diario íntimo'. This much has been confirmed by Carlos Gurméndez in his interview with Silvana Savini:

Ya en París me leyó algunos poemas; él hacía, como Unamuno, un poema diario, casi un diálogo consigo mismo, pero no como refugio desde lo exterior sino como vocación. Su tipo de poesía es especulativa pensante, inductiva, además del gran dominio de la forma poética y forma clásica que juntaba en un pensamiento. (Savini, p.14)

Nigel Dennis and Gonzalo Penalva Candela have considerably advanced the study of Bergamín's work through their involvement in documenting, editing, and creating a chronological assessment of it. This has been a mammoth enterprise given that Bergamín's occasional writings are scattered over Latin America, predominantly Mexico, and France and Spain. Nigel Dennis is gratified not only by the evident admiration in which Bergamín's critical work is held but also by the general recognition of the fact that his prose work is understood as poetic in nature. Nevertheless, he does express concern at the lack of any comprehensive study of Bergamín's thought and expression:

Sin embargo, el problema es que este gran entusiasmo por la obra en prosa de Bergamín no ha pasado nunca del elogio fragmentario, y sigue faltando un estudio detallado de su pensamiento y su expresión.[4]

Elsewhere Dennis voices a particular concern for the assessment and critical appreciation of Bergamín's poetry:

No existe ningún estudio de la poesía de José Bergamín. Cada colección que ha aparecido ha sido reseñada de un modo favorable y a veces inteligente, y en este sentido puede decirse que se han iluminado fragmentos de su obra en verso. Sin embargo, no se ha intentado ninguna evaluación de esta obra en su totalidad.[5]

The fragmentary state of criticism to date on Bergamín's work is directly related to the sheer breadth of his literary output. The question of genre preoccupies critics who seem to feel that it is crucial to prioritize a certain genre for Bergamín's work. Their own critical coherence is bolstered by the attempt to define Bergamín in generic as well as stylistic terms. So for instance, as I pointed out in the introduction, if critics step out of the escape route which deems Bergamín's work to be unclassifiable, they either find themselves describing his work within the limits of a single and often limited critical concept, such as Savater's stylistic 'juego absoluto' or Rafael Conte's stylistic 'ante todo un poeta', or they ascribe to Bergamín the qualities of a Renaissance man who masters all literary genres bar the novel:

La verdad es que Bergamín ha cultivado casi todos los géneros — ensayo, teatro, poesía, aforismo: crítica y creación paralelas —, aunque su reputación hoy se debe a su papel de 'prosista de la generación del 27.' La etiqueta es vaga y nada satisfactoria, y no cabe duda este papel suyo en la constelación de escritores de pre-guerra ha sido poco estudiado y mal comprendido, y creo que en el fondo Bergamín sigue siendo una 'incógnita por despejar'.[6]

As Dennis points out, this global assignation is 'nada satisfactoria', though I would dispute his suggestion that the low esteem in which Bergamín is held is because of a failure of critics and historians of his time to recognize his literary worth. Their willingness to proclaim their unconditional admiration of his work belies any postulation of an underlying vindictiveness informing their critical stance. The sins of omission which Nigel Dennis lists further on in his article are not so much of a deliberate nature as a natural result of the ready distinction made between poets and literary and critical writers in general:

> Como otros destacados prosistas de los años 20 y 30 (el mismo Espina, Antonio Marichalar, Benjamín Jarnés, Corpus Barga, César Arconada, Ernesto Giménez Caballero...), Bergamín ha vivido durante largos y demasiados años bajo la sombra de sus hermanos poetas, los que han monopolizado la atención de los críticos llegando así a desfigurar el sentido de toda una época, reduciendo su riqueza y variedad a un puñalado de obras escritas en verso. Como es natural, el interés y valor de la obra de Espina y compañía son discutibles, y el olvido en que yacen sus escritos (en ciertos casos por lo menos...) no se debe exclusivamente a los caprichos de la historia literaria o a la miopía de los profesionales de la crítica. (El mismo Bergamín escribió una vez: 'Tal vez hay algo más piadoso para los muertos que el recuerdo — el olvido'). Pero el caso de Bergamín me parece distinto. Las causas de su marginación son en gran parte extra-literarias: el exilio y la prohibición. (p.144)

The neglect Bergamín suffers, aggravated by the circumstantial reality of his actual exiles and his political marginalization, is, as Dennis says, a result of the critical assumptions of the era as regards the 'Generación del 27': that poetry constituted the vanguard of Spanish artistic production of the time.

Pedro Salinas cites lyricism as the defining feature of the first four decades of the twentieth century in Spain, though he is careful not to limit the scope of the poetic merely to poetry itself:

> Pues bien; para mí el signo del siglo XX es el signo lírico; los autores más importantes de ese período adoptan una actitud de lirismo radical al tratar los temas literarios. Ese lirismo básico, esencial (lirismo no de la letra, sino del espíritu), se manifiesta en variadas formas, a veces en las menos esperadas, y él es el que vierte sobre novela, ensayo, teatro, esa ardiente tonalidad poética que percibimos en la mayoría de las obras importantes de nuestros días.[7]

Significantly, this lyricism is not seen as exclusive to poetry but is rather a tonal characteristic of other genres, including the essay. In this sense Rafael Conte's definition of Bergamín as 'ante todo un poeta' accords with Salinas's analysis of the cultural climate of the time.

However, and more important I feel, is the necessity to concede the very real problem Bergamín poses in terms of generic definition. It is not unusual to find in the 'Generación del 27' poets who are also critics. One has only to look here at their record in academe, and at the success of the critical work of García Lorca, Cernuda, Salinas, and Guillén to verify this assertion. However, crucially, each of these poets who also worked as literary critics or who contributed to the literary vanguard debate, was first a poet and then a critic. Bergamín, on the other hand, was first a critic, contributing invaluably to the publication and assessment of the work of poets such as Alberti, Salinas, Guillén, García Lorca, Altolaguirre, Diego, Prados, and Cernuda.[8] Only later, much later, does Bergamín actually start to publish a prolific amount of poetry and only then, in the 1960s, would it have been appropriate to call him a poet.

I suggest that this fact alone has contributed to the problem of definition that has dogged critical assessment of his work to date.

Although in the light of modern literary theory, which challenges the easy distinctions between literary creativity and literary criticism, it becomes easier to situate Bergamín as a creative writer who is not implicitly undermined by his prominence as a literary critic, it is important to note that both Salinas and Bergamín refrain from making generic distinctions. Both writers prefer to focus on the defining characteristics of the sensibility of a period. What Salinas considers to be lyricism Bergamín sees as the propensity of poetic writing itself towards the transcendent, as a propensity to resist definition *per se*. This he sees as 'la trascendencia estética universal de Andalucía',[9] its idealism: 'El idealismo andaluz se afirma, vivo, infantil, casi recién nacido, eterno' (p. 75). For Bergamín this 'andalucismo universal' refers to Spain in general and to Spanish art in general. Importantly, this 'andalucismo universal' is to come to seem a feature of Spanish poetic creation which differentiates it from that of other European countries: 'Este "andalucismo universal" ha influido tanto en poetas, músicos o pintores nuevos — andaluces o no —, que es fácil reconocer su huella en cualquier caso' (p. 72). The aesthetic of transcendence, like Don Tancredo, is both universal and quintessentially Spanish, just as, according to Bergamín, the bullfight challenges death in a culturally specific and universally applicable way: 'El toreo no es español, es interplanetario.'[10]

Bergamín's denomination of art, and of Spanish art in particular, as that which has a propensity towards the transcendent points to a rejection of definition *per se* simply because the notion of transcendence itself devalues the very concepts of definition and distinction as we ordinarily understand them. Joseph Campbell clarifies this point in *The Power of Myth*:

But 'transcendent' properly means that which is beyond all concepts. Kant tells us that all of our experiences are bounded by time and space. They take place within space, and they take place in the course of time. Time and space form the sensibilities that bound our experiences. Our senses are enclosed in the field of time and space, and our minds are enclosed in a frame of the categories of thought. But the ultimate thing (which is no thing) that we are trying to get in touch with is not so enclosed. We enclose it as we try to think of it. The transcendent transcends all of these categories of thinking. Being and nonbeing — those are categories. The word 'God' properly refers to what transcends all thinking, but the word 'God' itself is something thought about.[11]

Bergamín's avowed search for the indefinible in art logically poses critical problems for his work, given that he enacts his belief not only in his own poetry but also in his literary criticism. When a critic attempts to make generic or historical reference to Bergamín's work, the substance of that work militates always against the critic's sphere of reference. Typically, Bergamín's spiritual orientation in the materialist, modern world threatens to transcend all critical thinking, at least in terms of easy categorization. Furthermore, Bergamín's own avoidance of discursive self-expression deliberately scuppers such easy categorization.

POETIC VALUE AS SPIRITUAL VALUE

Carlos Gurméndez's mention of Unamuno in his characterization of Bergamín's poetry as a 'diario íntimo' throws further light on the difficulty of situating Bergamín's work from a generic point of view. Bergamín never sanitized his esoteric and hermetic style into the novel form, unlike Unamuno, so, whilst he shares many existential concerns with Unamuno, he never presents his intimate personal stuggle in a discursive, novelistic form. His views are thus never more palatable than in his theological tracts and, later on, in the 'diario íntimo' of his poetry.[12] I would contend, therefore, that the tardiness of the publication of Bergamín's poetry, and the hermeticism of the poetry itself, have militated against the acceptance of the poetic nature of his other writings. His work has not been generally considered to be that of a poet first and only secondly as that of a literary and cultural critic, simply because the reverse proposition has, at first glance, much truth in it.

Furthermore, it is the resistance of Bergamín's work to generic definition, the breadth of his output, and the confusingly poetic analytical style of a man who is not publishing poetry, which has produced a certain critical resistence to placing Bergamín in the 'Generación del 27'. Indeed, at the first sign of any purely creative urge, such as *Caracteres* (1926) or the early aphorisms, *El cohete y la estrella* (1923) and *La cabeza a pájaros* (1925-30), critics leap to the defence of Bergamín precisely as a poet. When Salinas speaks of Bergamín's aphorisms he suggests that the purpose of the aphorism is that of creating poetic value:

Así, por ejemplo, en este libro: fijémonos en el título, *La cabeza a pájaros*; en el título de la última parte, *El grito en el cielo*. Son fragmentos de dos frases hechas: 'tener la cabeza a pájaros', como indicando ser aturdido y ligero, y `poner el grito en el cielo', quejarse extremadamente. Y, sin embargo, dentro del lenguaje bergaminiano, estas dos frases separadas de los verbos que, por decirlo así, les sirven como de asa o mango por donde todos las han empuñado hasta ahora, *cobran un valor de poesía, exenta de toda servidumbre en la vida del lenguaje: son una cosa nueva.*[13]

Salinas connects the poetic value of Bergamín's aphorisms to the spiritual source of his preoccupations:

El ingenio de Bergamín en sus verdaderos momentos es solamente el arma punzante, acerada, con que un espíritu atormentado y angustiado quiere abrirse paso entre las tinieblas de cada día. (p. 164)

Salinas sees the tormented, anguished imperative of Bergamín's aphorisms as the impulse which informs the poetic. The poetic and the spiritual nature of the aphorisms is precisely what differentiates them from the 'ingenio y agudeza' of a Gracián or the practical, social truths of a La Rochefoucauld:

Pero este ejemplo nos lleva justamente a otra cuestión, que es la diferencia del aforismo bergaminiano con lo que este género suele ser. No busca Bergamín las verdades prácticas; su meta es la verdad poética. (p. 164)

So, for Salinas, not only is Bergamín a poet but he is a poet because of his trembling revelation of human anguish:

Así, Bergamín es en realidad más que un acuñador de frases que contengan una filosofía práctica de la vida, un revelador de visiones poéticas, y su pensamiento como el del poeta, es 'un arte de temblar', según él mismo titula una parte de su libro. Su obra es casi siempre la obra de un poeta gnómico. Ese es el valor del arte de Bergamín. (p. 164)

Salinas sees the predominance of lyricism in the twentieth century as a stylistic change of pace in the arts, a move away from the nineteenth century:

El pensamiento de Bergamín no se presenta en forma discursiva y extensa, ensayos largos o artículos, al modo de la generación anterior: un Unamuno, un Ortega y Gasset. Hay sin duda que insertarle en el mismo linaje de preocupados o de atormentados espirituales, pero con muy profundas diferencias en cuanto a la tonalidad del pensamiento y a la calidad artística. *Ha habido en el siglo XX en toda Europa algo como un cansancio de las dimensiones normales, una busca de velocidades y de ritmos que se apartaran de la andadura del siglo XIX.* (pp. 159-60, my italics)

For him, this change of pace manifests itself in two distinct forms: the excessively discursive and the fragmental expression of the quintessential. He places Bergamín in the second of these poetic styles:

Ese anhelo se ha expresado por dos caminos: uno de ellos, lo hipertrófico, el desmesurado extenderse de una obra artística, como en el caso de Proust, Joyce, entre otros. La contraria es la fragmentación del pensamiento, el 'quintaesencismo', la ambición de la brevedad y de la concisión para reforzar los efectos. Bergamín se encontró, desde luego, del lado de la quintaesencia y contra el fárrago. (p. 160)

It is perhaps because the first of these forms is considered to pertain to the novel and because the lineage of tormented writers carves a direct path to Bergamín that Salinas sees him as fitting into the second of his categories, his more discursive work being viewed as crucially influenced by spiritual documenters such as Unamuno. Written in 1934, Salinas's essay suffers from an obvious lack of awareness of the sheer abundance of Bergamín's later extensive essays. However, his analysis of writing in the twentieth century as essentially lyrical encompasses both stylistic spheres. The lyrical inheres in all genres and in all of Bergamín's writing. Salinas, in this sense, accurately affords Bergamín the status of visionary, describing his style as a 'proceder por iluminaciones' (p. 160) and thus echoing Juan Ramón Jiménez's portrayal of Bergamín in 1922 as someone who could capture unedited ideas:

Yo decía: *¡Qué largo y qué delgado, qué estirado se está poniendo José Bergamín!* Era el tercer estirón, el definitivo, para llegar con la mano a esa capa finísima, casi incolora ya del aire, donde están las ideas inéditas.[14]

The wish for genre distinction, evident even in Salinas's work, is disguised as something other than a purely critical tool. The fixing of definition in this way, whether concerning genre, style, or the notion of artistic movements, though critically expedient, often fails to elucidate not just because it is too specific but because it is too general. However, we have seen that the generalization of the fragment against the discursive in Salinas's analysis of Bergamín leaves the reader stuck in a possibly false dichotomy which does not account for the multiplicity of genres in which Bergamín, at least nominally, works. His drama, for example, is not so much dramatic as philosophical and poetic, and his critical essays are literary but seek to break down a false distinction between the critical and the creative.[15] Indeed, this sort of expediency in thought is one of Bergamín's fundamental preoccupations, a concern that the urge to make distinctions does not become a source of obfuscation rather than elucidation. Poetic discourse is a privileged discourse for Bergamín precisely because it is aware of the problem of definition and struggles with the constraints of the intellect and of language.

Bergamín had an acute sense of the folly of excessive definition, aware as he was of the insufficiency of the intellect to explain and contain reality, whether that be nature or culture. In his essay '¿Qué es poesía?', which contains, significantly, ruminations around Bécquer's maxim 'Poesía eres tú', poetry as the territory of otherness, Bergamín suggests that poetic discourse attempts to take account of the elusive nature of reality and the obfuscatory role of intellectual definition. For him, poetic vision should militate against definition since definition, the imposition of the rational human mind, misreads the nature of reality. Ultimately he points, in his allusions to Novalis, to the potential of poetry to dissolve the categories of rational and temporal definition as the essence of poetry itself:

'Existe un presente espiritual — pensaba Novalis — que identifica el pasado con el porvenir, disolviéndolos. Y éste es el elemento esencial del poeta, su atmósfera propia'. Y también: 'la poesía disuelve todas las demás existencias en su existencia propia'.[16]

The poetic task for Bergamín is one which recognizes that intellectual structures create the conditions for escape from all that is ephemeral or immaterial, capturing only what is merely material, and distorting and killing even that. Although intellectual grids or paradigms help us to apprehend reality, at the moment at which they become unconscious they become dangerous, as fatal as a spider's web. Bergamín uses an analogy to describe how we perceive reality:

Cuando miramos al cielo con telescopio, nos decía un filósofo novelista, ponemos en la lente que nos lo aproxima a la mirada una red de constelaciones que nos definen las estrellas para poder contarlas. (p. 181)

Our definition of reality quickly becomes indistinguishable from the apparent form of reality: 'A veces, sucede que olvidamos que fuimos nosotros quienes, entre el cielo y nuestros ojos, habíamos trazado esas líneas finísimas sobre el cristal para comprenderlo' (p. 181). When we draw the defining lines of reality, we are in effect making a judgement about the world, hence the juxtaposition of the concepts of 'definición' and 'juicio' in Bergamín's analysis: '¿Qué tiene que ver esta tela o telar dudoso de nuestro juicio, o juicios, con aquella red invisible de definiciones que proyectamos sobre el cielo?' (p. 181). The urge to know, implicit in the attempt to define what we see, is a continual questioning of the reality of what we see, 'como si la pusiéramos en duda' (p. 181). And at root this questioning is a matter of life or death, itself a truth that we have forgotten: 'Olvidando la reminiscencia palabrera de la tela o tela que fue el campo de la justa caballeresca o del juicio de Dios' (p. 181). Like the root of the popular expression, we forget that the jousting-field challenges death and that God's judgement decides between death and immortality.

In effect, what we capture in the web of our understanding, we imprison and kill:

¿No serán, una y otra, red, tejido o tela, parecida a la que llamamos del mismo modo que tejen las arañas? ¿Y de análoga finalidad, la de cazar moscas? ¿Como tela o telas de araña son las redes que teje nuestro juicio para aprisionar con ellas las cosas? ¿Y qué cosas, qué realidad, no se nos escapa de tal sutil y leve prisión con la que envolvemos? (p. 181)

What we capture, or imprison, we kill. The spider's web, coming as it does from within the spider, is an extension of its physical reality, its body. It spins a web in order to consume the fly, and this for the spider is a necessary relationship to reality and at a physical, immediate level a challenge to death, an act of survival. Our relationship to reality is similar to that of the spider and the fly. Reality exists for us to consume, or at least we make this connection as we both exist and consume, and yet reality, things, are also more than that. We project our understanding onto reality and yet our understanding is partial. This is the way things must be: a spider is dependent on the air, on the insufficiency of the web to catch the fly, and so it is with our understanding. Our understanding is precisely this: an understanding of the way our intellect orders and describes what we do not understand because it lies beyond us, just as the spider spins out of its body and into the beyond. To mistake our understanding for reality would obscure a deeper pattern of which we would become unaware, and for Bergamín it would be fatal for us to be so unaware because our self-consciousness is entirely dependent upon our consciousness of this 'más allá'.

Just as the spider has a necessary relationship with its external circumstances, similarly, it must be remembered, the eternal realm of poetry depends upon a dialectical relationship with its temporal oppressor, history:

Y esta realidad absoluta en que tiempo y cosa se juntan, ¿es la poesía? 'La poesía y la historia, todo puede ser uno', había afirmado nuestro Lope. Y Holderlin: 'La poesía es el fundamento que sostiene la historia': la palabra en el tiempo (canto y cuento es la poesía). Palabra no gastada. (p. 203)

Of course, as Bergamín suggests, language itself responds to the demands of cursive time and from language comes the utopian poetic of eternity:

This linear time is that of language considered as the enunciation of sentences (noun + verb; topic - comment; beginning - ending), and that this time rests on its own stumbling block, which is also the stumbling block of that enunciation — death.[17]

For Bergamín, the catalyst of poetry which seeks transcendence is the material world of the non-transcendent: the temporal condition of estrangement, of death makes explicit an anguish which a utopian vision alone would veil. Bergamín, then, appears to agree with Kristeva's view of the temporal restrictions of language when he implies that the importance of poetic discourse lies in language's simultaneous disavowal of and desire for eternal time. This much he makes clear in '¿Qué es poesía?', in his analysis of Machado (p. 202).

The necessary dialectic I have been outlining between cursive time and eternity is for Bergamín a prerequisite for the creative urge.[18] However, its appearance as a trope in his poetics and as a fundamental part of his religious sensibility has done much to befuddle the discussion of Bergamín's own historical place as a member of the Generation of 1927. This is because he does not totally reject historical categories, despite the fact that he is concerned to ensure that historical categories are not given undue importance.

The fact that Bergamín implicates himself so totally in the search for the ineffable disrupts critical debate around his place in the Spanish artistic panorama, whether that debate involves his generic and stylistic nature or his historical relevance to the 'Generación del 27'. He is, in a sense, always writing from a perspective that is, with some exceptions, dissimilar to that of his commentators. The attempt to instate Bergamín into the 'Generación del 27' poses the problem very neatly as one of history against eternity. Given that temporality itself is the scourge of Bergamín's existential outlook, it is hardly surprising that temporally fixed definitions as regards any writer, including himself, are only useful to him, as a critic, in a limiting historicist sense. This platitude becomes problematic of course only if, as in the case of Bergamín, such a platitudinous critical concern blinds the reader to the central concerns of the writing itself: a placing in time which disguises the urge to step out of the constraints of time.

Bergamín does not appear to reject historical fact when it concerns only that, since, for instance, he is happy to accept his historical involvement with the 'Generación del 27':

Ahora se habla mucho de generaciones, y constelaciones literarias y está muy de moda hablar de la 'generación del año 1927', en la que se me incluye supongo que por razón de verdad. Al principio creí que debía protestar, y no de que se me incluyera, que eso es inexorable como diría Azorín, sino de la elección del año 27 como fecha significativa cuando precisamente esa fecha no tiene ninguna significación. Al fin he creído comprender que esa fecha es legítima por insignificante; como si al aplicarse a esa generación, a la que sin duda pertenezco, se quisiese subrayar con ello su insignificancia. Naturalmente la modestia me obliga a la conformidad.[19]

Here Bergamín makes it obvious that the designation 'Generación del 27' is simply a convenient, though largely vacuous, label for a group of writers. So, although he felt some need to protest at the title 'Generación del 27', he would not dispute his own involvement with the community of writers to which the label refers. His objection is as ever to the temporalization of that which he considers to function out of time, namely art. The historical existence of the generation itself should, he believes, be known more appropriately as the 'Generación de la República', since it refers to the politically real:

A esa que decimos mal llamada *generación del 27*, y a la arbitraria selección de nombres que con ella se hace, creemos, como Antonio Espina, que habría que llamarla *generación de la República*, o en todo caso, de la Dictadura (por partida doble: por las dos dictaduras andaluzas, la política y la literaria, particularísimas las dos). Preferimos llamarla la de la República, porque aunque su vida literaria coincidiese con los años que corren entre el veintitrés y el treinta y seis — sus dos fechas históricas importantes — culmina con la última, cuando la guerra la desbarata y dispersa.[20]

He considers the 'Generación del 27' to be a label which functions in a literary sense as a 'promoción', a definition which suggests not only a group but also a type of self-advertisement. In his eyes such a 'promoción' should not be mystified. Literary development, historically speaking, is contorted and misrepresented if such definitions are applied too rigorously: Bergamín quite clearly espoused a more general overview of culture. Such an overview would seek always a point of comparison rather than merely difference. However, this is not to say that difference and distinction are disregarded.

The sense of differentiation Bergamín seeks is of a poetic order, one which escapes history, which escapes the trap of temporality:

La poesía existe porque se determina o define a sí misma críticamente, situándose, o sea, relacionándose: y esta relación, puramente, exclusivamente poética — no histórica ni psicológica — , no es de semejanza, sino de diferencia: no hay relación ni definición posible, que no sea: diferenciación.[21]

Bergamín's critical work in this sense refers always to a poetic realm which refuses to function within the scope of traditional literary criticism. He is quite simply speaking of something of a different order. This different order is the realm of the poetic, the realm of 'eternal presence', ('el presente eterno'). It is deeply self-reflexive and it refers always to a spiritual continuum whose task it is to challenge the temporal and reach towards the transcendent. The notion of a spiritual continuum does have a historical reality but it is far more wide-ranging and general than the concern for the definition of generations or vanguard movements. So, for instance, rather than discussing the existence and relevance of the 'Generación del 27' or Surrealism in literary terms, Bergamín's concern is to situate the work of the writers of an 'edad de plata' in a continuum with the 'edad de oro'. He does this by laying claim to the 'eternal presence' of Góngora: Góngora is significant in 1927 not because he is being commemorated but because he is 'actual'. Bergamín refuses to rank the poetic relevance of Góngora within a temporal framework when he is referring to Góngora's effect upon contemporary poets:

El arte poético de Góngora vale hoy, para los nuevos, porque es arte y porque es poético; nada más; otros paralelismos no existen; si no es el de la verdadera intención estética que anima, como a Góngora, a los poetas del nuevo renacimiento lírico.[22]

Contemporary poets, also, are only recognized by Bergamín in terms of their place on the spiritual continuum. They are, like Góngora, eternally present:

Toda obra poética verdadera — realizada — es actual siempre — esto se quiere decir cuando se dice que es inmortal o eterna —. De la actualidad, — o actuación poética — de

Góngora, da testimonio, durante tres siglos, como ahora su presencia, su permanencia; suscitando siempre entusiasmos y hostilidades. (p. 48)

It is crucial to note here that when Bergamín posits the existence of an eternal poetic realm he also posits a notion of differentiation that functions within that realm. He can therefore distinguish different poetic voices such as those of Bécquer, Guillén, Alberti, and Cernuda according to a system, a spiritual, poetic yardstick which subordinates historical linear considerations to the sidelines. So he values poets according to their ability to escape the constraints of the literary formulas of their time. He is not positing a Bloomian notion of the anxiety of influence so much as a process of utopian desire, that of consuming mortality to gain eternal life. By this I mean that although Bécquer's strength lies in his difference from Spanish Romanticism, Bergamín sees this differentiation in terms of Bécquer's ability to approach 'la obra poética absoluta'[23] rather than in terms of the forging of literary immortality: 'El acierto de Bécquer fue limpiar, encalar — constantemente — la turbulencia de una pasión romántica. Su distancia del romanticismo español es esa: su distinción' (p. 80). This is an illusion of transcendence that Harold Bloom would read as individuation but which Bergamín would see as a refusal to be tarnished by linear time, the expression of the desire for transcendence without objectivization such as I outlined in the opening chapter of this study.

If, as I suggest, Bergamín judges literary production according to a spiritual continuum, the details of historical analysis become instruments only of embellishment to his study, details that cloud the deeper imperatives of the poet's work. In this context Bergamín hastens then to compare Alberti to Bécquer, for both exalt 'la obra poética absoluta':

'Entre santa y santo, pared de cal y canto.' Entre el poeta y la poesía no hay relación viva: no hay sombra de pasión, de enamoramiento. No hay erotismo sensual, ni sentimental. Se levanta un muro, una pared infranqueable: de imperativa, limpia, pura castidad. Pared de cal y canto. La obra poética absoluta. (p. 80)

Interestingly, the individuality of the poet is disregarded and the relationship of the poet to his work is elided to make space for the poetic work which occupies an eternal space.[24]

THE CHRISTIAN POETIC REALM

Underlying Bergamín's aesthetics of an eternal poetic realm is an implicit consciousness of a distinction between immortality and eternity or eternal life in the Christian sense. Crucially, eternal life in Christian terms implies the resurrection not just of the soul but of the body, a consideration which has repercussions for the Christian perception of material reality. In the first edition of *Cruz y Raya*, alongside Bergamín's own 'El pensamiento hermético de las artes', Alejo Revilla, in his article 'El cristianismo y los misterios del mundo greco-romano', points out the distinctive nature of eternal life in relation to Graeco-Roman, pagan notions of immortality: 'Inmortalidad, idea esencialmente distinta del concepto cristiano de vida eterna.'[25] The notion of resurrection is, according to Revilla, particularly alien to pagan culture: 'Los diferentes medios que nos han transmitido las tradiciones míticas no proporcionan tampoco fundamento sólido para hablar de resurrección' (p. 94).

Revilla's conclusion seeks to distance any reading of Christianity in terms of a pagan mythical culture and certainly this reading is biased, with the portrayal of the Christ story as fact rather than fiction. Bergamín himself is much less defensive about Christian doctrine. His poetry, as we shall see, admits to the appeal of Christianity partly on the grounds of the way it answers the need or desire not to die in human terms, which could be considered the root of pagan as well as Christian ideology. However, his attitude to poetry and temporality is, in the final analysis, closer to Revilla's vision simply because Christianity is perceived as providing for the eternal life of man rather than for the immortality of the gods, the salvation of man, through the crucifixion and resurrection of Christ. As Revilla concludes:

La idea de un dios que padece, muere y resucita para comunicar a sus fieles la vida eterna, no existe en ninguno de los misterios paganos. Profundamente extraños, por su espíritu a las doctrinas cristianas, los mitos, que hemos analizado brevemente, no admiten parangón, ni siquiera en su letra, con la sencillez del *mensaje pascual* evangélico y paulino: Jesús de Nazaret, por nuestros pecados crucificado bajo Poncio Pilato, muerto y sepultado, *ha resucitado realmente y hase aparecido a Simón Pedro.* (pp. 97-98)

The insistence on an eternal, newly born poetic realm inheres in the Christian notion of eternal life rather than in the notion of immortality. Bergamín's vision of a spiritual continuum is entirely dependent on a Christian sensibility which regards the wish to transcend death as a wish to achieve eternal life rather than immortality in Bloomian or pagan terms. His claims for the extemporaneous potential of poetry constitute not so much a disavowal of mortality as an account of the process of desire which seeks an eternal realm, denied to, but envisaged by the poet. He seeks in poetry the conflation of the human and the divine, the possibility of seeing the eternal from the perspective of the temporal. I shall show how Bergamín achieves this conflation by admitting the reality of corporeal mortality to the process of continual renewal. Bergamín puts the body back into the spirit: his notion of transcendence pivots on a vision of sacrament and sacrifice which makes it possible for him to talk about eternal life without regarding it as disembodiment into a merely spiritual immortality. So his spiritual reality, the continuum he seeks in other poets, is the: 'Confluir natural de toda poesía verdadera: poesía nueva, recién nacida, hambrienta de cosas, de ideas: de realidad espiritual.'[26] This spiritual reality, though seemingly ineffable, functions, paradoxically, in a Christian context as a process of consumption; sacrifice and sacrament, a dialectic of harmonization, of the body and the soul in time, in order to envisage the eternal: 'Y así es, según clamaba Dante: lo que *más sangre cuesta*. La imaginación es carnívora: se alimenta de sangre, no de sueños' (p. 87).

For Bergamín, then, poetry concerns man's ability to cope with the material, his ability to consume and transform materiality: 'Canto hondo, preso entre dientes. Como la boca de un animal en un cuerpo vivo hace presa en las cosas el blanco afán duro de la poesía. Canto y cal' (p. 83). Material reality is sacrificed on a poetic sacramental altar. The material enters into a dialectic with its own mortality. Bergamín's own poetry is about death because it is about the realm of the transcendent, about God. Poetry is the same place, the situation of 'cal y canto', as Bergamín supposes for Alberti's poetry:

El canto de ese andaluz muro encalado que Alberti levanta en su poesía, corta en dos mitades el mundo: este mundo y el otro; este mundo, el del pensamiento, el de la poesía: mundo aparte y a partes de razón y pasión iguales. Doble juego. Separación perfecta. (Sombra y sol). Pared de cal y canto. Porque lo que hay a los dos lados del muro simultáneamente, no lo ve más que Dios. (p. 84)

The poet's task, like the task of sacrifice and sacrament, is one of purification; the search for the transparent realm: 'Alberti lo adivina y repite el verso becqueriano: *huésped de las nieblas*: de las nubes; casta, pura limpia, luminosa atmósfera celeste: la más clara, tenue y fina transparencia' (p. 81). This vision of transcendence is conditioned by the notion of physical as well as spiritual purification, a mystical zone of suffering and resurrection, rebirth. The poetic realm is envisaged though never reached, and the beauty of poetry is the telling of the poet's baptismal passion, his struggle to end his exile from that which 'no lo ve más que Dios' (p. 84). Bergamín continues:

La poesía exige hasta la crueldad blanquísima de su transparencia (niebla escandinava de Bécquer, eterno hospedaje poético), quemarse en ese fuego casto, duro, amargo, de la cal viva. La poesía de Alberti choca contra la luz de su empeño inmaculado de nitidez para que la imaginación poética, entre sombra y sol (cal y canto), proyecte sus realidades puras: construcción alba, angélica, de la poesía: su aurora. (p. 85)

Bergamín seeks to stress the humanity of poetry along with the anthropological nature of religion. For, though the realm of poetry is the realm of transcendence, the task of writing poetry is the realm of human endeavour, the endeavour not to die. Ortega y Gasset's art without transcendence would be inhuman, so art with transcendence would be human. Bergamín seeks the material in the spirit because he seeks the humanity in transcendence. In this sense, Ortega's assumption that art without transcendence dehumanizes art would be logical, but in Bergamín's terms undesirable and impossible. Bergamín bases his criticism of Ortega on the fact that the latter´s theory of art should make modern art antipopular, which for Bergamín is clearly not the case, as he suggests that the new art is indeed applauded by the public:

En los estrenos que hemos presenciado en Madrid del 'Pájaro de fuego' y de 'Petruchka' la mayoría — la totalidad del público —, unánime y entusiasmado, admiró y aplaudió, sin que hubiera una sola protesta.[27]

The essential humanity of poetry is the defining quality of what Bergamín calls 'poesía de verdad'. For Bergamín it is the humanity of Salinas's *La voz a ti debida* that appeals to him:

Por eso, esta poesía tiene razón de ser, es verdadera: porque tiene razón de ser humana, o sea, razón de ser moral. Es ésta la tradición más firme de la poesía, la de la poesía amorosa, en el sentido moral, o racional, y, en definitiva, humano. [...] Poesía de verdad. De verdad, no de vida, y sí debida a ella, a su verdad humanísima: y que por serlo, tan de veras, lo es, como lo es del hombre, tan humana: debida a la mujer. Esa voz, humana, desnuda, verdadera, de la poesía eterna es la que nos habla en este libro, quizá el mejor de Pedro Salinas, en este poema magistral.[28]

The humanity of poetry, rather than being the flaw of poetry, is an essential part of the dialectic Bergamín perceives in the poet's task. This is similar to Guillén's rejection of Ortega's analysis of modern art:

Si hay poesía, tendrá que ser humana. ¿Y cómo podría no serlo? Poesía inhumana o sobrehumana quizás ha existido. Pero el poema 'deshumano' constituye una imposibilidad física y metafísica, y la fórmula 'deshumanización del arte', acuñada por nuestro gran pensador Ortega y Gasset, sonó equívoca. 'Deshumanización' es concepto inadmisible, y los poetas de los años 20 podrían haberse querellado ante los Tribunales de la Justicia a causa de los daños y perjuicios que el uso y abuso de aquel novedoso vocablo les infirió como supuesta clave para interpretar aquella poesía. Clave o llave que no abría ninguna obra.[29]

According to Bergamín, the impossibility of escaping the human, the description of this pain, was the content of the poetic task of Juan Ramón Jiménez. This is the song of mortality which Bergamín sees as the legacy of Romanticism and which he compares to the death throes of the 'calamar' which when it has exhausted its venom, spews out its own life blood in an illusion of life which is in fact its death. As he observes in 'Poesía de verdad':

Toda una poesía, un esteticismo poético, nos dio este espectáculo, se nos dio en esta bella y angustiosa exhibición mortal de su agonía viva. Como el calamar. El calamar recién pescado que, agotada su tinta defensiva, al escupirla, ofrece con su sangre, transparentándola cristalinamente en todo su ser por la congestión de la asfixia, una agonía coloreada infinitamente, como un crepúsculo. Esta ilusión de vida que es expresión de muerte fue la de aquel esteticismo, ilusoriamente poético, cuando quiso salir afuera, al aire libre, a la verdad. (p. 90)

Juan Ramón Jiménez sought the sublime through his own narcissism, refusing to partake in the dialectic between the human and the divine, the body and the spirit, seeking transcendence from a human perspective of the vision of eternity, as divine, in poetry itself. He sought to possess poetry as a woman, refusing to recognize the limitation of the human, seeking to constitute his immortality by means that would not admit the limitations of the human, would not leave the woman, poetry, in the realm of the poetic and the divine. Thus, in 'Poesía de verdad', Bergamín states that:

Esa poesía fantasma, sin principio ni fin, en permanente fuga, pudo prolongarse indefinidamente, diluyéndose más y más en su propio inmoralismo poético, su amoralismo esteticista. Y toda esta obra poética, ilusoria de vida, de su autor, es su prolongación, en efecto, agónica, crepuscular; sus ecos, sus reflejos; es la supervivencia, cada vez más debilitada, de aquella inmoral, por sólo bella, idolatría, de aquel perecedero, a fuerza de querer inmortalizarse orgullosamente por sí solo, narcisismo suicida. Fue así el esteticismo puro, la imagen invertida, mortalmente, hasta el fondo de su espejismo, por aguas corrompidas de tan mansa quietud, y de la inquietud cenagosa de sus ranas. Del hervidero, que dijo el profeta de sus ranas. Y a este hervor o fervor renacuajo se fue alambicando aquella poesía hasta ofrecer ya únicamente, destilada, una pureza absoluta, desvivida, inhumana, venenosa, mortal. Con 'voz velada' por la muerte. (p. 91)

What Bergamín is referring to here is the idea that the modern is mistaken in its view of the potency of man. Man can only partake of the transcendent by rendering respect to the divine nature of the transcendent and by admitting the impossibility of denying his mortality in human terms. Juan Ramón Jiménez's mistake can be seen as that of trying to become a god, trying to become immortal, rather than trying to gain eternal life in human terms. The realm of the poetic is the place where man can enter into a dialectic with the divine only by conceding the otherly nature of the divine. Poetry in this sense is feminized for the male poet, but feminized iconographically. The cosmic nature of Salinas's beloved, her 'más allá', allows her to be synonymous with poetry itself, gives her transcendence. Salinas's relationship with the beloved is of interest to Bergamín precisely because it is a relationship. This relationship is dialectical: she creates Salinas and Salinas worships her by creating her anew as poetry. Conversely, Juan Ramón Jiménez recreates the virgin muse in order to defile her with his phallic pen. The relationship between the human and the divine is infected and dismantled by his narcissism. The person of the poet, the mortal scribe in Juan Ramón Jiménez, offends Bergamín, whereas Salinas renders respect to the voice of 'J' (as Bloom would have it), to the divine as envisaged by the partial human eye. The divine/human dialectic consumes and is consumed by poetry in a continual sacrificial process of renewal.[30] It is in this context that Bergamín challenges the definition of the modern, setting up his own yardstick.

LA ESTATUA DE DON TANCREDO

As I suggested at the beginning of this chapter, Bergamín's notion of art suffers the same misreading as does his literary persona. He considers all true art to be a common quest for transcendence, so that great art is not a statement of individuality but a facing up to death. All art is poetic for Bergamín and all poetics face up to, challenge, death. Again, the reason for this is religious or to do with faith. Reason dictates our death, faith challenges death and seeks immortality. So, for Bergamín, poetry is anti-rational. He extrapolates this idea in *La estatua de Don Tancredo*. Don Tancredo pretends to be a statue of himself in the bullring: he pretends to be immortal by re-creating himself as art. He goes out of himself and becomes other, and yet lives the fallacy of this; in this sense he lives the struggle/contradiction between faith and doubt, immortality and death:

Y así da el paso decisivo de su vida: el de la inmortalidad; decide disfrazarse de estatua para vencer la muerte desafiando al destino; o sea que, según nuestro hombre, no basta con hacerse el muerto para ganar la vida, para salvar la vida, sino que hay que ir más allá todavía: hay que hacerse inmortal, hacerse el inmortal: disfrazarse de estatua. (pp. 83-84)

The image of the statue is particularly pertinent:

Entonces tropieza con algo que es más inmóvil que la misma muerte; algo que se queda quieto de un modo mucho más definitivo: la estatua. (p. 83)

This vision of the quietude and potential immortality of statuary is reminiscent of the ancient Egyptians, who believed that sculptors were the guardians of immortality:

Belief in the power of the image was probably the reason that Egyptian sculptors made effigies of the dead. The image was believed to guarantee survival after death. Bazin tells us that, in the Nile valley, 'the sculptor was known as "He-who-keeps-alive"'.[31]

Don Tancredo's statue is both incantatory and primitive; alluding to the magical potential of art to create the immortal and to a social, anti-individualist notion of art which pertains both to Bergamín's vision of art and to the artistic views of primitive societies.[32] Bergamín rejects the modern because of modernity's refusal to concede a place to the transcendent. Don Tancredo, in contrast, remains faithful to a vision of transcendence: 'Y así es, o se hace, encarnación visible y trascendente de la totalidad de nuestro ser, ante la vida, por la muerte, y *ante la eternidad de lo probable*, por el azar; en definitiva ante Dios' (p. 79). His statue challenges the estrangement and solitude of human existence, challenges death in his encounter with the divine: 'Un hombre solo; pero no vacío, sino lleno de su vacío, pleno de soledad: solo ante el toro, ante la muerte; solo, por eso, por todo eso, plenamente solo, ante Dios' (p.79).

Don Tancredo's statue also elides the difference between the poet and the poem. Don Tancredo distils the passion for immortality rather than creating an object of immortality, unlike the Eiffel Tower, his point of comparison, which speaks only of death in its Modernist allegiance to materialism:

La Exposición francesa ante el novecientos era el enorme bazar de todo aquel mundo o feria de vanidades que el esqueleto de la torre Eiffel ha perpetuado mortalmente; porque este esqueleto de hierro no es un esqueleto que pueda esperar la resurrección. [...] Toda aquella modernidad o modernismo de bazar ardía artificiosamente en la quemazón del siglo nuevo, dejándonos en pie, clavada, como el esqueleto quemado de esa gran rueda de toda fortuna secular, el testimonio permanente de lo muerto. (pp. 75-77)

For Bergamín, it is precisely the singularly materialist nature of the Eiffel Tower which condemns it to its vacuity:

Si desafía al tiempo, lo hace por haberle entregado su carne totalmente [...] Hay cielos en los que su cenicienta expresión se hace tan patética que verdaderamente nos perpetúa, vanamente piramidal, la forma mismo del vacío, de la nada, de la muerte eterna. (p. 76)

The equation of modernity with mortality, with a disturbing rejection of the notion of transcendence, with spiritual bankruptcy, emerges mainly as a religious concern in the first four decades of the twentieth century, and the problem of Christianity for Bergamín is one typical of his time: he is concerned with maintaining a notion of transcendence in a world that is becoming increasingly materialist. Jacques Maritain, writing for Bergamín's *Cruz y Raya*, expresses this fear in the following way when talking in 1935 about the avant-garde artistic movements of the early twentieth century:

La situación efectiva del arte del momento ha cambiado enteramente de quince años a esta parte. ¿Hay algo más pasado de moda que el cubismo? El angelismo pictórico y poético parece completamente acabado. Un arte que se negaba la contemplación, una inteligencia que se quería sin ningún instante de pasividad, fabricante pura de mundos y formas, confiesan su vacío a fuerza de actividad — el vacío natural del intelecto humano cuando *lo otro* no penetra su vida —. A fuerza de elevarse por la sola virtud de la ligereza y la agilidad en las alturas prohibidas, al fin se aperciben que no tienen peso. Este arte, como el héroe de Chamisso, ha perdido su sombra.[33]

For Maritain, as for Bergamín, art which does not concern itself with transcendence can testify only to the vacuity of human existence. Whilst accepting the political necessity of social upheaval, Maritain fears the misalignment of the social over the spiritual, the clouding of human fragility by the supremacist doctrines heralded in the name of progress. For instance, he sees Gide's communism as a historical trap with which the temporal concerns of humanity threaten to cast the atemporal concerns of humanity into a perilous oblivion. For him, as for Bergamín, this constitutes an erroneous disregard for 'lo otro':

Mas hemos de volver a nuestro tema, que se refiere al instante 1935. Sea lo que quiera la significación de la adhesión de Gide al comunismo en relación con su propia persona, la misma adhesión constituye un síntoma importante de la primacía ejercida dondequiera actualmente por lo social y de la renuncia del arte ante los cuidados y angustias del momento presente. (p. 297)

The equation of modern art with mortality, with a vitalist, individualist tradition, is not however merely a Christian concern for the twentieth-century religious thinker. It implicates both the religious and the non-religious. Like George Steiner, Bergamín would see the absence of the divine as proof not of the new realism of the modern age but as a dangerous oblivion of the relevance of the transcendent. Instead of assuming that 'vacant metaphors, eroded figures of speech, inhabit our vocabulary and grammar', Steiner puts forward the idea that:

Any coherent understanding of what language is and how language performs, that any coherent account of the capacity of human speech to communicate meaning and feeling is, in the final analysis, underwritten by the assumption of God's presence.[34]

Steiner goes on to suggest that the experience of aesthetic meaning in particular implies the necessary possibility of God, of what he calls 'real presence'. In his study he contends that:

The wager on the meaning of meaning, on the potential of insight and response when one human voice addresses another, when we come face to face with the text and work of art or music, which is to say that when we encounter the *other* in its condition of freedom, is a wager on transcendence. (p. 4)

Steiner's assignation of transcendence, though in many ways merely a philosophy of common sense which rejects solipsism, is similar to Bergamín's view in its insistence upon the need to imagine the 'necessary possibility' of God as a prerequisite for the creation of art. In *La estatua de Don Tancredo* Bergamín criticizes Modernism's implicit assumption of the irrelevance of such concerns. The distinction he is at pains to make is that between the illusory creation of something that is immortal and the poetic figuring of the quest for immortality, such as that which Don Tancredo enacts.

What differentiates Steiner's conjecture from Bergamín's is the figure of Christ as the substantiator, the mediator between man and God, the assumption that the realm of the divine is anthropological in the sense that it is Christian. The divine is accessible because of the measure it yields to humanity. Bergamín's attack on what he considers to be the illusions of modernity radiates from what he sees as the appalling absurdity of talking about man as if the transcendent were merely illusion. Bergamín's reaction to Nietzsche is informed by the same conviction that Steiner expresses: 'Grammar lives and generates worlds because there is a wager on God' (p. 4). However, Nietzsche's work came as a flash of enlightenment to Bergamín not because God was dead but because he was dead to man.

Bergamín's attitude to the modern is that of a man who refuses to oust the idea of God and sees the modern as itself illusory because it pretends to man's self-importance and self-sufficiency. What would be interesting to Bergamín about Derrida's lost transcendent signifier is not the inappropriateness of searching for the transcendent, based on the assumption of its non-existence, but rather the fact of loss, a loss of vision for man, the loss of man's ability to perceive the divine rather than the loss of the divine itself. The masks of language display the futility of human expression but still hide the promise of meaning and function on the 'wager on God'. So poetry becomes a catalogue of loss, and Bergamín's own poetry can be seen primarily as a process of mourning, as Kristeva describes, which implicitly challenges a sense of loss:

We find ourselves here before an enigmatic chiasmus that will not cease to preoccupy us: if loss, mourning, absence set the imaginary act in motion and permanently fuel it as much as they menace and undermine it, it is also undeniable that the fetish of the work of art is erected in disavowal of this mobilizing affliction.[35]

The poet, in this sense, is always a visionary for Bergamín because the poet's task is one of unveiling the transcendent:

Pero el arte poético nace, se desentraña — porque es vivo— de la oscuridad, de la más profunda oscuridad: de la honda mina entrañable y laberíntica en que el poeta, a imitación de la naturaleza, engendra de su propia sangre espiritual, de su propia sustancia lírica, la visión fantástica o imaginativa: su intuición bella universal, a imitación de lo divino, que da a luz, viva — y dolorosamente — la forma poética. Esta forma poética — arte poético, prosa y verso, poesía pura, — es el *poema*, y existe fuera de toda otra realidad por sí misma — y para sí misma — por sí sola. La sola realidad poética es la poesía; la acción y la pasión poéticas tienen sus razones propias — razón única — de existir: la razón poética.[36]

It is for this reason that Bergamín distinguishes so forcefully between the 'moderno' and the 'nuevo', which is the eternally newly born. Bergamín envisages temporality as something to flee and contends that art as an immortal monument still implies temporality.

THE PRIAPIC COMPLEX

The Priapic complex, or rather the inappropriately inflated credence accorded to phallocratic discourse in the twentieth century, sheds some light on the confusions surrounding the artistic impulses of the era.[37] Indeed, the Priapic complex often blinds the artist to the distinction between the creation of something that is immortal and the poetic figuring of the quest for immortality. The former is an example of the dominant male ego or the phallus, whereas the latter empowers the divine/feminine, the powers that are beyond the human/masculine. Bergamín's lauding of *La estatua de don Tancredo* over the Eiffel Tower not only indicates his discontent with the materialist modern world, but also gestures to an awareness of Priapic inflation in the processes of symbolization, in aesthetics.

Bergamín's grappling with the notion of time, foregrounding as it does his dialectics of Faith, is underpinned by his implicit assumption that the modern rejection of transcendence is also a rejection of the feminine. He tries to realign such an imbalance through his assertion of the continued relevance of the concepts of rebirth, eternity, and in the Christian sense, resurrection.

Julia Kristeva clarifies the ways in which particular concepts of time have been associated with the binary symbolic categories of the masculine and the feminine. Like Bergamín, her contention is not that linear time is an erroneous concept of time or even that linear time has been falsely masculinized: rather it is that the weighting of culture towards masculine or phallocratic values has pushed aside two other concepts of time that are associated with the feminine. Toril Moi, in her comments on Kristeva's 'Women's Time?', distinguishes between cyclical and monumental time, which are associated with female subjectivity, and linear time which is the time of history:

According to Kristeva, female subjectivity would seem to be linked both to *cyclical* time (repetition) and to *monumental* time (eternity), at least in so far as both are ways of conceptualizing time from the perspective of motherhood and reproduction. The time of history, however, can be characterized as *linear* time: time as project, teleology, departure, progression, arrival. This linear time is also that of language considered as the enunciation of a *sequence* of words.[38]

Kristeva, like Bergamín, recognizes that the human condition forces a continual confrontation between the temporality which designates human mortality and the consciousness of another eternal time, monumental time, which feeds the wish for transcendence:

In other words, we confront two temporal dimensions: the time of linear history, or *cursive time* (as Nietzsche called it), and the time of another history, thus another time, *monumental time* (again according to Nietzsche), which englobes these supra-national, socio-cultural ensembles within even larger entities. (p. 189)

The cyclical and monumental concepts of time, symbolized as feminine, are of particular relevance to religious sensibility. The fact that they are linked to a maternal female subjectivity does not render them fundamentally incompatible with masculine values or patriarchal culture:

The fact that these two types of temporality (cyclical and monumental) are traditionally linked to female subjectivity in so far as the latter is thought of as necessarily maternal should not make us forget that this repetition and this eternity are found to be the fundamental, if not the sole, conceptions of time in numerous civilizations and experiences, particularly mystical ones. (p. 192)

Kristeva associates these feminine notions of time with the matrix-space or 'aporia of the *chora*' (p. 191), a space which is 'nourishing, unnameable, anterior to the One, to God and, consequently, defying metaphysics' (p. 191). Her idea is reminiscent of Bergamín's feminine principle of faith, alluded to in the three sonnets of Chapter 1. Specifically, the feminine religious principle is recalled, for Kristeva, in the resurrection myths of various religions:

Or one is reminded of the various myths of resurrection which, in all religious beliefs, perpetuate the vestige of an anterior or concomitant maternal cult, right up to its most recent elaboration, Christianity, in which the body of the Virgin Mother does not die but moves from one spatiality into another within the same time via dormition (according to the Orthodox faith) or via assumption (the Catholic faith). (p. 191)

Here, the concepts of time which are linked to the feminine are also those which are linked to the idea of transcendence, of the escape from mortality, and to the Christian doctrine of the resurrection. It seems that when Bergamín grapples so insistently with the complex and paradoxical manifestations of time, he is doing so within the arena of his specifically religious sensibility, through a poetic discourse which, as Kristeva suggests and Bergamín appears to exemplify, rests upon the linguistic stumbling-block of enunciation in linear, passing time, — upon death (p. 192).

Finally, the relationship between art and temporality is played out in Bergamín's own poetry and most forcefully in his poetry on death, which will be the focus of the next chapter. Here, I shall consider Bergamín's poetry as a process of mourning, as a cathartic accommodation to Loss: loss of life, identity, meaning, and utterance. And in her essay 'On the Melancholic

Imaginary' Kristeva eloquently describes the figuring of a perspective which accords with that of Bergamín:

Aesthetic — and, in particular, literary — creation, as well as religious discourse in its imaginary fictional essence, proposes a configuration of which the prosodic economy, the dramaturgy of characters and the implicit symbolism are an extremely faithful semiological representation of the subject's battle with symbolic breakdown.[39]

NOTES

[1] José Bergamín, *La estatua de don Tancredo*, in José Bergamín, *El arte de birlibirloque. La estatua de don Tancredo. El mundo por montera* (Santiago de Chile and Madrid: Cruz del Sur , 1961).

[2] Francisco C. Lacosta, 'Al margen de los clásicos: José Bergamín', *Hispania*, 50 (1967), 54-62 (p. 54).

[3] See bibliography.

[4] Nigel Dennis, 'El neobarroquismo en la prosa española de pre-guerra: El caso de José Bergamín', *Cuadernos Americanos*, n.s. 5 (September -October 1984), 144-61 (p.146).

[5] Nigel Dennis, *El aposento en el aire: Introducción a la poesía de José Bergamín*, p. 15.

[6] Nigel Dennis, 'El neobarroquismo en la prosa española de pre-guerra: El caso de José Bergamín', p.144.

[7] Pedro Salinas, 'El signo de la literatura española del siglo XX', in Pedro Salinas, *Literatura española siglo XX* (Madrid: Alianza, 1983), pp. 34-45 (pp. 34-35).

[8] See examples of Bergamín's critical work on these poets in José Bergamín, *El pensamiento de un esqueleto: Antología periodística I*, ed. by Gonzalo Penalva Candela (Málaga: Litoral , 1984).

[9] José Bergamín, 'El idealismo andaluz', *La gaceta literaria* (June 1927), reprinted in Penalva Candela, *El pensamiento de un esqueleto: Antología periodística I*, pp. 72-75 (p. 72).

[10] José Bergamín, *El arte de birlibirloque* (Madrid: Turner , 1985), p. 72.

[11] Joseph Campbell, with Bill Moyers, *The Power of Myth*, ed. by Betty Sue Flowers (New York: Doubleday, 1988), p. 62.

[12] See, for example, Bergamín´s *El pozo de la angustia* and his *El clavo ardiendo*, with a preface by André Malraux, 2nd edn (Barcelona: Aymá, 1974).

[13] Pedro Salinas, 'José Bergamín en aforismos', in *Literatura española siglo XX,* pp. 159-64 (pp. 162-63), my italics.

[14] Juan Ramón Jiménez, 'José Bergamín (1922)', in *El cohete y la estrella/La cabeza a pájaros*, ed. by José Esteban (Madrid: Cátedra, 1981), p. 43.

[15] See, for example, Bergamín's, *Los filólogos* (Madrid: Turner, 1978) and his *Beltenebros y otros ensayos sobre literatura española* (Barcelona and Madrid: Noguer, 1973).

[16] José Bergamín, 'Las telarañas del juicio - ¿Qué es poesía?', in *De una España peregrina*, pp. 179-203 (p. 203).

[17] Julia Kristeva, 'Women's Time?', in *The Kristeva Reader*, ed. by Toril Moi (Oxford: Blackwell, 1986), pp. 186-213 (p. 192).

[18] 'Esta ecuanimidad de alma, por serlo materialmente de tiempo, de tiempo material, le sigue acercando a nuestros clásicos, que lo son por vivificarse y verificarse de este modo en el tiempo y por él; singularmente de aquellos en quienes esa corriente temporal — 'palpitación de espíritu' — asciende como el surtidor de la imagen bergsoniana de la evolución creadora.' (¿Qué es poesía?, p. 202).

[19] José Bergamín, 'El panorama literario', *Sábado Gráfico* (April 1975), reprinted in *El pensamiento de un esqueleto: Antología periodística I*, pp. 63-67 (p. 65).

[20] José Bergamín, 'Pasemos la página', *Sábado Gráfico* (December 1977), reprinted in *El pensamiento de un esqueleto: Antología periodística I*, pp. 68-71 (p. 70).

[21] José Bergamín, 'La poética de Jorge Guillén', *La Gaceta Literaria* (January 1929), reprinted in *El pensamiento de un esqueleto: Antología periodística I*, pp. 76-79 (pp. 76-77).

[22] José Bergamín, 'Patos del aguachirle castellana', *Verso y Prosa* (June 1927), reprinted in *El pensamiento de un esqueleto: Antología periodística I*, pp. 47-49 (p. 48).

[23] José Bergamín, 'El canto y la cal en la poesía de Rafael Alberti', *La Gaceta Literaria* (March 1929),

reprinted in *El pensamiento de un esqueleto: Antología periodística I*, pp. 80-87 (p. 80).

[24] In this article Bergamín sees eroticism as extremely problematic and, for instance, rejects Juan Ramón Jiménez's eroticization of the muse as erroneous because it obstructs the poet's vision of the poetic by making the muse too earthly. He wants to keep the muse in the realm of the transcendent, keep her otherly and feminine in terms of transcendence rather than in terms of the objectivization of the body of woman. In this sense the poet steps back from his individuality as a poet, ultimately disowning his work and portraying it as residing in the supremely generous realm of the gift, the realm of the divine, less part of himself than a part of God.

[25]. Alejo Revilla, 'El cristianismo y los misterios del mundo greco-romano', *Cruz y Raya*, 15 April 1933, 67-99 (p. 87).

[26] José Bergamín, 'El canto y la cal en la poesía de Rafael Alberti' , p. 82.

[27] José Bergamín, 'Criba', *España* (January 1924), reprinted in *El pensamiento de un esqueleto: Antología periodística I*, pp. 40-44 (p. 41).

[28] José Bergamín, 'Poesía de verdad', *Luz* (January 1934), reprinted in *El pensamiento de un esqueleto: Antología periodística I*, pp. 89-93 (p. 92).

[29] Jorge Guillén, 'Apéndice: Lenguaje de poema, una generación', in Jorge Guillén, *Lenguaje y Poesía*, 3rd edn (Madrid: Alianza, 1983), pp. 181-97 (pp. 190-91).

[30] See Harold Bloom, *Ruin the Sacred Truths: Poetry and Belief from the Bible to the Present Day* (Cambridge, MA: Harvard University Press, 1989), p. 3.

[31] Anthony Storr, *Solitude* (London: Flamingo, 1989), p. 76.

[32] On the latter, see Storr, Chapter 6, pp. 73-84, and in particular pp. 75-77.

[33] Jacques Maritain, '¿Quién pone puertas al canto?', *Cruz y Raya* (April 1935), reprinted in '*Cruz y Raya*': *Antología*, pp. 295-316 (p. 295).

[34] George Steiner, *Real Presences* (London and Boston, MA: Faber and Faber, 1989), p. 3.

[35] Julia Kristeva, 'On the Melancholic Imaginary', in *Discourse in Psychoanalysis and Literature*, ed. by Shlomith Rimmon-Kenan (London: Methuen, 1987), pp. 104 -23 (p. 105).

[36] José Bergamín, 'Notas para unos prolegómenos a toda poética del porvenir que se presente como arte', *Verso y Prosa* (August 1927), reprinted in *El pensamiento de un esqueleto: Antología periodística I*, pp. 109-14 (pp. 112-13).

[37] For a detailed analysis of the Priapic complex, see James Wyly, *The Phallic Quest: Priapus and Masculine Inflation* (Toronto: Innercity Books, 1989). In particular, Wyly stresses the effect of the Priapic complex upon the functioning of the symbolic: 'There is no sense of metaphor, no receptivity to symbol, no ability to fantasize, not even an openness to analogy or simile. Everything is concrete, and is exactly what it is. *Phallos* is phallus is intercourse is flesh-and-blood orgasm — exclusively. The denial of the symbolic, and therefore of the psychological, is total' (p. 71).

[38] Julia Kristeva, 'Women's Time?', pp. 186-213 (p. 187).

[39] Julia Kristeva, 'On the Melancholic Imaginary', in *Discourse in Psychoanalysis and Literature*, pp. 109-10.

CHAPTER 3

THE THEME OF DEATH IN THE POETRY OF JOSE BERGAMIN

THE SUBJECT'S BATTLE WITH SYMBOLIC BREAKDOWN

In this chapter I shall examine how Bergamín's poetry tries to enact a battle against death, how his poetry is always concerned with death, and how language and the body are the creators of metaphor. The body is the most material reality we know, and yet it is destined to disappear. For Bergamín, therefore, images are masks of reality: they delude us into putting our allegiance into the material world which is transient. We live in a demonic world: the images are the so-called reality we see around us, but these images are not transcendent reality. Thus the death of the images around us is not a real death and the death of the material body which is the ultimate image is not death either. For Bergamín, poetic language is two-sided, both hermetic and Orphic.[1] It is only poetic discourse which can reveal a reality beyond the material world. Paradoxically, the language of poetry has bodily potential: the death of the body allows the transcendent nature of body to be revealed through resurrection in religious terms and through a process of 'desengaño' in poetic language which aims to unveil the hidden, hermetic potential of the process of representation. So whilst Bergamín's poetry represents what Kristeva terms 'the subject's battle with symbolic breakdown' in the face of death, it also seeks to resolve such a symbolic breakdown through the espousal of a poetic dialectics of faith, through a dialectical balance between the 'Orphic' and the 'hermetic' sides of the world and language.[2] Such a dialectic both mourns and mitigates mortality for Bergamín.

Nigel Dennis has observed that:

Los escritos de Bergamín — los más auténticos, los más sentidos — eran algo así como una consecuencia de sus meditaciones íntimas sobre la presencia constante y el insondable misterio de la muerte.[3]

Here he underlines the fact that the whole of Bergamín's literary career was coloured by his preoccupation with death. The theme of death, with its physical imminence and its unknowability, was to influence profoundly Bergamín's belief in immortality, his philosophical attitudes towards life, and ultimately his confidence in the possibility of articulating such central human concerns in language. For Bergamín, the implications of the unknowability of death were both mirrored in and enacted by language, itself prone to the same existential problems with which it grapples; permanence and mutability.

It must be noted from the start that, as a Christian, Bergamín was committed to the concept of Logos, which privileges the Word within a totalizing vision of a monotheistic universe. From his Christian standpoint, Being and the Word are coupled and designated in the one concept: Logos. The concept of death, however, was to continually destabilize Bergamín's belief in Christianity. Death seems to contradict from a rational point of view the doctrine of immortality, signalling as it does a contingency in human existence which is dictated by Man's apparent finality. If Being is to persist, as Christian doctrine suggests, through the Word made Flesh, then language must cease to designate Man's mortality and, instead, reveal a bodily potential for eternity. Bergamín's poetry can be seen as a search for such bodily potential in a language which apparently contradicts the notion of a 'transcendental signified', hemmed in as it is to the temporal reality, and thus the mortality, it seeks to escape.

Resolution and indeed salvation are sought through the figure of Christ. In the prologue to the first issue of *Cruz y Raya* (April 1933), the editors, among whom Bergamín numbered, affirmed their Christian orientation: 'Para nosotros, *la definición esencial* del espíritu tiene un nombre: Cristo.'[4] The notion of the potentially eternal spiritual essence of Christ challenging the apparent transience of the body was later to become the root of many of Bergamín's depictions of his own consciousness as ephemeral, insubstantial, and yet paradoxically enduring. The spectre of death, the finality of Man's consciousness in continual conflict with his existential purpose, the urge to encompass the infinite, informed and shaped the work of Bergamín and that of his companions in *Cruz y Raya*. It is important to note the following statement from the prologue to the first number of *Cruz y Raya*:

Nos afirmamos por una rectitud voluntaria de nuestra finalidad espiritual: en este sentido, que es el de la línea, la del linaje católico de nuestro ímpetu. (p. 10)

Given that Bergamín accepted the concept of Logos, identity and utterance were to become bound together in an uneasy union in his world view. Both notions, his logocentrism in effect, the assumption that there is an essential truth in the material world, and that this 'metaphysics of presence' holds sway also in language, were called upon to answer the implications of death, immortality, faith, and doubt with a similar and interdependent urgency. The centrality of these preoccupations in Bergamín's writing caused Dennis to define him as an 'escritor *agónico*'.[5] This is a definition confirmed by the critical stance of the editors of *Cruz y Raya*, among whom Bergamín figured most prominently. They endeavoured to 'situar críticamente su pensamiento, para ponerle, y ponerse por él, en verdadera situación crítica: en angustiosa, por verdadera pasión de espíritu: en espiritual, verdadero apuro'.[6] Bergamín's angst was imbued with a sense of urgency, 'verdadero apuro', which reflected his conviction of the proximity of death:

> Cuántas veces huyendo de la muerte,
> escuchabas sus pasos en tu sueño,[7]

It also revealed a concern to maintain a tension between faith and doubt in the system of Christian belief, with statements such as 'la duda y la fe son el ritmo vivo del pensamiento' and 'La certeza es el enemigo de la fe'.[8]

This faith/doubt dialectic translates itself into the urgent anguish so often associated with a Christian sensibility informed by the existentialist tendencies of the day (taken on not least of all by Unamuno, an early mentor for Bergamín), a sensibility which designated anguish as a prerequisite for ethical integrity:[9] 'Por eso nos afirmamos por la cruz, negándonos con ella.'[10]

For Bergamín, the necessary instability of his belief in Logos, in God, constantly threatened yet constantly renewed by doubt, was continually manifest in the reality of death. Therefore, the theme of death was to constitute a referent, unknowable and so absent, imminent and so ever-present. This referent or yardstick became a pivot for his ethical, critical, political, and aesthetic views. Death was the one certainty which challenged his non-referential, transcendent signified: Logos.

Death is ever-present in Bergamín's work, beginning with the ghosts and skeletons of his early plays, *Tres escenas en ángulo recto* (1925) and *Enemigo que huye* (1927), and continuing through his critical writings such as *Fronteras infernales de la poesía* (1959) and *Beltenebros* (1973), right up to his culminating poetical work of the last three decades of his life, with *Esperando la mano de nieve* (1985) and his final *Hora última* (1984). Bergamín felt, as did Cervantes, that 'en todo hay cierta, inevitable muerte' (*Poesía, I*, p. 29), and that the proximity of death succeeded in blurring the distinction between life and death:

> Siento la muerte tan cerca
> que me parece que el alma
> dormida no la sintiera.[11]

The presence of death was so intense as to be inexpressible in all but paradoxical terms:

> Como si se despertara
> de su sueño en otro sueño
> en el que no sueño nada.
>
> (*Poesía, IV*, p. 53)

In *Del sentimiento trágico de la vida* Unamuno suggests that Man's essence is wholly shaped by the wish to surpass death:

Es decir, que tú, yo y Spinoza queremos no morirnos nunca y que este nuestro anhelo de nunca morirnos es nuestra esencia actual.[12]

Thus, he posits that Man's central preoccupation is that of immortality:

Quiero decir del único verdadero problema vital, del que más a las entrañas nos llega, del problema de nuestro destino individual y personal, de la inmortalidad del alma. (p. 28)

Unamuno then adds that, for this reason, the idea of God became necessary:

Para sustentar esta inmortalidad aparece Dios [...] que Dios para la generalidad de los hombres es el productor de inmortalidad. (p. 29)

According to Unamuno, Christianity brings together two traditions: the Greek and the Judaic. The former espouses a belief in the immortality of the soul and the latter espouses the resurrection of the flesh. The resurrection of the flesh was brought about in history in the person of the Christ:

Pero luego que murió Jesús y renació el Cristo en las almas de sus creyentes, para agonizar en ellas, nació la fe en la resurrección de la carne y con ella la fe en la inmortalidad del alma. Y ese gran dogma de la resurrección de la carne a la judaica y de la inmortalidad del alma a la helénica nació a la agonía en San Pablo, un judío helenizado, un fariseo que tartamudeaba su poderoso griego polémico.[13]

In *La agonía del cristianismo* the agony of Christianity is specifically a bodily agony centring not only on the immortality of the soul but also on a faith in the resurrection of the flesh.

For both Unamuno and Bergamín, the wish not to die and the hope for eternal life are seen as Man's prime motivations. Bergamín, however, is not so much concerned with the philosophical understanding of these motivations as with the investigation of the impact of the desire for immortality on his identity. His ontological security is seemingly undermined by his desire to transcend a rational, mortal sense of self.

MORTALITY AND IDENTITY

The problem of personhood which I examined in Chapter 1 is acted out in Bergamín's poetry. The urge to partake of a transcendent reality challenges the notion of identity which inheres in the material world, which is circumscribed by the rational knowledge of death. The failure of the material world to subscribe to the concept of Logos undermines the validity of the modern concept of identity by defining such identity as estrangement or loss. Consequently, the paradoxical figuring of identity as loss, or lack of definition in the material world, such as that described in the following poem, can be seen as a positive statement in favour of a personhood which desires to persist beyond the material world in a transcendent realm:

> Puedo sentirme vivir
> sin pensar que estoy viviendo,
> como si mi vida entera
> lo fuera fuera del tiempo.
>
> Puedo, huyendo del sentido,
> escapar al pensamiento
> sin sentir y sin pensar
> si estoy vivo o estoy muerto.
> Puedo parecer que soy
> y no ser lo que parezco.
> Puedo dormir y soñar
> que me despierto en un sueño.[14]

The idea that life is an illusion of life is dependent upon the desire for another, greater life beyond the constraints of mortality. The experience of life as mortal, though, is a source of anguish to Bergamín, and this experience of a selfhood which is transient, but which is nevertheless the only verifiable sense of Self, is to become the catalyst for the description of both the anguish of his mortal state and the desire to transcend it. Like most utopian desires, the description of Bergamín's escape from estrangement radiates from a denial of the validity of his lived reality towards an affirmation of a desired vision. Much of his poetry is a repeated reiteration of, on the one hand, a cathartic mourning of loss and, on the other, a statement of potential: 'Puedo parecer que soy / y no ser lo que parezco.' The continual juxtaposition and even conflation of these two attitudes promotes, as Nigel Dennis claims, the dialectics of faith which foreground Bergamín's poetic utterances:

En sus mejores momentos él es siempre poeta, y lo que escribe, lo que crea, resiste al análisis lógico y racional. Sólo a través de la nueva lógica de la fe — a través de una lectura sentimental y poética de sus libros — podemos apreciar las profundas verdades *disparatadas* que contienen.[15]

The transcendence of Self implies an elision between Self and otherness which further resists the notion of identity as it is experienced in the material, mortal world. Again, the conceptual tools of Bergamín's material existence cause an anguish of estrangement in him which impels him to seek the dissolution of his sense of Self in favour of a merging with otherness as it manifests itself to him either as earthly, in the form of woman, or as divine. Ramón Gaya recognizes this poetic conceit as, paradoxically, a form of self-preservation for Bergamín:

Peut-être aussi parce qu'être confondu avec d'autres nous protège, nous préserve, nous épargne, mieux encore nous permet d'être ce que nous sommes intensément et au coeur de nous-mêmes; être confondu avec un autre nous maintient intact, non contaminé, à condition évidemment d'avoir la force d'affronter la pure et inhumaine solitude où nous abandonne cet échange.[16]

Bergamín's poetry on death, then, can be seen as both a deliberate annihilation of the specific sense of Self which would condemn him to the partiality of a material existence and also as an anguished description of the experience of life as merely that, as singular, isolated, mortal, and insufficient.

So intense is Bergamín's preoccupation with death that it undermines the value of life itself. There is no 'burning to the socket' for the poet, for death does not intensify his vital experience; death is too pervasive and invasive:

> La vida tendría sentido
> si traspasara la muerte
> con su sentir dolorido:
>
> un sentir de lo vivido
> que fuese mucho más fuerte
> que el recuerdo y el olvido.

> (*Poesía, IV*, p. 55)

Desires, hopes, and fears are seemingly irrelevant when one is faced with the certainty of death and so, consequently, is the mysterious, contingent nature of life and personal identity. The paraphernalia of identity, the landscape of memory and oblivion, and the wish not to die are irrelevant when death, though so close, is so unknowable as to be indistinguishable from life itself.

This pervasive sense of death in life casts doubt over not only Bergamín's vital experience but also, by extension, over the representational tools that his Christian sensibility traditionally employs to describe the realms of life and death. For instance, the fear of Hell is meaningless since it cannot be conceived; a greater fear being the void:

> Si le temes a la muerte
> no es porque temes a Dios
> ni al Diablo: lo que temes
>
> es muchísimo peor;
> temes no encontrar en ella
> a ninguno de los dos.[17]

Bergamín's concern is not so much whether eternal life exists or whether his belief in God or trust in Christ are misplaced, but rather he is concerned with his suspicion that it is impossible to apprehend such ideas with any success:

> A la vuelta del camino
> la muerte te está esperando.
> Tú parece que lo sabes
> y vas andando despacio.
>
> La sorpresa que te aguarda
> es que la vas a encontrar
> como si no la encontraras.

(Poesía, IV, p. 49)

They are ideas that are forever out of reach:

> Las que me importan
> son cosas que no tienen
> vuelta de hoja.

(Poesía, VII, p. 89)

Here his desire is for an escape from a binary affirmative/negative articulation which is identified with a non-human, that is divine, page with no other side. The implicit suggestion is that the binary distinctions of rationality are somehow dependent upon the notion of death. The notion of death creates an unanswerable rift in human experience and conceptualization between life and death, and sets in motion the affirmative/negative constructions of rational discourse. I shall investigate the implications of this idea in my discussion of Bergamín's notion of the Fall in Chapter 4, however at this stage it is important to note that Bergamín's wish to overcome such binary articulations informs his attitude towards death. One might even suggest that his poetic elision of the distinction between life and death, his insistence on the pervasive presence of death in life, constitutes a radical attack on the restrictive perceptions of mortal humanity. His refusal to accept such a partial vision is dependent upon a desire to perceive something more, to perceive the divine, and glimpse the possibility of eternal life. Paradoxically, such negative ruminations on death ultimately shore up a vision of eternal life because they attempt to erode the power of death over the human imagination. In his essay 'El pensamiento hermético de las artes' he opposes a vitalistic view, restricted by humanity, to his plea for a vision of Logos.[18] For, according to Bergamín, if one cannot gesture towards the possibility of a 'true' apprehension of Logos, of the 'verdadera situación crítica', the bridge between life and death becomes a difference without distinction:

> – ¿De dónde vienes?
> – No sé
> – ¿A dónde vas?
> – Lo sospecho.
> – ¿Y a dónde sospechas ir?
> – Me figuro al Infierno.
> – ¿No temes estar ya en él?
> – Es lo que me estoy temiendo.
> – ¿Y sabes por qué lo temes?
> – Sé que no quiero saberlo.
>
> *(Poesía, VII*, p. 36)

Thus, much of Bergamín's poetic technique is founded upon the subversion of common distinctions between the accepted categories of Being and Non-being as he attempts to topple the hegemony of the existential certainty of death and replace it with a creative faith/doubt dialectic.

The uncertainty expressed in the previous poem highlights the insufficiency of the traditional dichotomy between Being and Non-being. Indeed, Bergamín frequently makes a mockery of Man's attempts at an all-encompassing vision with his aphoristic oppositions, subverting the discourse with his trite but tragic vacuity:

> Creo que cuando estoy vivo
> lo estoy porque no estoy muerto.
> Todo lo que es positivo
> es negativo primero.
>
> *(Poesía, VII*, p. 34)

He can only counter his anguished uncertainty with a diabolic creed, echoing the Catholic one. In the same vein, at other times he posits a logical paradox and then ridicules it with an infantile echo:

> Tengo que negarme a mí
> para afirmar que soy yo.
> Para que sea que sí
> tengo que decir que no.
>
> *(Poesía, VII*, p. 34)

Bergamín is faced with the physical certainty of death and the unknowability of death, a paradox which causes him to question the validity of all of his expressions of being, all utterance, and his relationship to the world and others. He remains ambivalent to ordinary conceptual structures and yet is forced to treat them as valid, simply because he has no other recourse:

> Iba sembrando semillas
> de ideas y pensamientos:

> se las comían los pájaros,
> se las llevaban los vientos.

(Poesía, VII, p. 93)

The articulation of this ambivalence is rooted in his sense of dislocation from Self:

> No ven ya por mí mis ojos
> lo que creen estar mirando:
> lo que escuchan mis oídos
> no lo oyen ya al escucharlo.
> Hasta el corazón y el alma
> se me están volviendo extraños:
> me siento dentro de mí
> de mí mismo separado.[19]

He indulges in internal dialogues with a positive alter-ego which has the very resources he is denied:

> Si yo soy una sombra,
> tú eres el fuego.
> Y si eres una voz del aire,
> yo apenas eco.

(Poesía, VII, p. 101)

This is despite the fact that his concept of otherness lacks definition apart from the most elemental, essential features of fire or air, with the voice of air, for instance, lacking individual utterance or substance. Bergamín consequently remains the reduction of an already negative or lacking definition:

> Yo soy hoy el que no soy,
> porque soy el que no fui:
> mañana seré ¡ay de mí!
> el mismo que no soy hoy.

(Poesía, VII, p. 85)

Just as he is an 'esqueleto vivo' (Poesía, VII, p. 65), an illusion of life, whose only definition is the most irreducible physical attribute, the skeleton, so too the external world becomes a place of shades, of half-lives:

> Los árboles son tan altos
> y tan largos los caminos
> que el paisaje se convierte
> en fantasma de sí mismo.

Y no se sabe, al mirarlo
de sí mismo desvivido,
si es desensueño del alma
o ilusión de los sentidos.

(*Poesía, VII*, p. 98)

Time becomes an illusion, which, when unmasked, leaves no comfort in the valley of death: the past, paradoxically, becomes proof of non-existence, rather than of life:

¡Ay! Aquellas horas muertas
se fueron quedando todas
enterradas en los ecos
de sus campanas sonoras:

(*Poesía, II*, p. 13)

The sense of death has accompanied Bergamín since the day he was born and its continual presence stops him from being able to penetrate the reality of other people:

El día que yo nací
nació conmigo una sombra
que no se aparta de mí.

Una sombra que por sí
y de sí misma se asombra
y me separa de ti.

(*Poesía, VII*, p. 99)

Bergamín's inability to objectify the Other, himself, or the world provokes a profound sense of weariness and isolation in him as he wanders through life:

Como si fuera una sombra
por este parque sombrío
voy andado, solitario,
sus solitarios caminos.

(*Poesía, II*, p. 12)

This even denies him the power over his own steps, 'voy andado', his weariness being translated into a sense of powerlessness. Bergamín comes to doubt his very existence and even mocks himself for such a delusion:

Los dos creemos
que somos, ¡ay!, lo mismo
que si no fuéramos.

(*Poesía, VII*, p. 101)

Even the logic of paradox cannot contain or express his anguish. He turns to double negatives which not only re-enact his distance, or dislocation, from a sense of Self, but also distance him from the reader:

> Vivir es un soñar
> desensoñando sueños.
> Morir es despertar
> para desensoñar
> un solo sueño eterno.
>
> (*Poesía, VII,* p. 89)

Death, although the only certainty, remains indescribable, and logic or reason is necessarily subverted and mocked:

> Tanto generalizar
> acaba por no ser nada.
> Nada de particular.
>
> (*Poesía, VII,* p. 86)

So, with such triteness, even death becomes insignificant, especially when Man's apprehension of the divine is condemned to the limitations of human thought, and Man is consequently condemned to the illusion of life which, though doubted, cannot finally be unmasked. Only the gap between consciousness and death seems appropriate to the half-life of existence: absolutes dissolve into dream, sleep, oblivion, shadow:

> Si no hay Diablo no hay Dios.
> Y si no hay Dios no hay Diablo.
> Sólo gracias a los dos
> podemos vivir soñando.
>
> (*Poesía, VII,* p. 87)

ESCAPING THE TYRANNY OF SELFHOOD

Given that selfhood constitutes a delusion, created by the illusion of material plenitude, and given that death most intensely signifies the annihilation of the Self, Bergamín attempts to escape the tyranny of this erroneous sense of Self through what appears to be a paradoxical affirmation of estrangement, through the figuring of true material selfhood as lack, or diminishment, or illusion. Bergamín cannot step out of his own metaphysics, cannot objectify himself, so he displaces himself, in continual mirrorings which, so he hopes, may leave traces of an apparently ungraspable Essence. Hence his half-life actually defines itself as partial:

> Mi sombra no es sólo una sombra,
> es un asombro de ser
> sombra de una lucecita
> que ya ha dejado de arder.

(Poesía, VII, p. 92)

Although Bergamín seems here to negate his existence, he restrains himself from any absolute negation and affirms at least a past existence, also ironically negated in the paradox. The vestiges, however, he acclaims as a life-force, though a residual life-force: he even ascribes a life-force to death, despite the essential contradiction of death's essence:

> Estoy sintiendo mi muerte
> temblar en todo mi cuerpo:
> porque es mi muerte quien tiembla
> cuando yo la estoy sintiendo.

(Poesía, VII, p. 92)

This life-force, this tremor, which is expressed as physical, reflects Bergamín's eternal paradox of death as the defining force of the Self, but of a Self which is a pale reflection of another, desired, transcendent, and therefore self-consuming Self. The effect is confusing because, again, Bergamín has only his limited human experience and language with which to describe his projections of the eternal, the non-human, the divine. Imagistically, he returns to corporeal or elementary imagery to describe the divine, groping his way towards articulation through paradox. Bergamín creates a mythical landscape where Man wanders between the divine world of God and the human physical world of the Earth: Man oscillates midway between these two, debarred both from his natural environment, by his will to escape its fatal implications, and from the world of the gods, by his humanity. Bergamín's anguish is further intensified because the human world is demonic in nature: it has human and divine features. This fact makes him more intensely aware of his loss of the divine. However we shall see that, eventually, it is precisely the demonic nature of poetic language, its divine potential, which allows the poet hope in a partial resolution of his predicament. Most of the time, though, he wanders in a half-world of blurred distinctions, neither general nor particular, populated with insubstantial beings, fragments, and projections of his fragmented Self: ghost, shades, flickers of dying lights, and the will-o-the-wisp demons of debilitated desire:

> Esa sombra que se alarga
> a mi lado, yo no sé
> si es mi sombra o mi fantasma:

(Poesía, IV, p. 14)

Bergamín is subject to the tyranny of differences without distinction, where he is forced to contemplate the ineffectual nature even of metaphor, which continually fails to accrue meaning.   An example would be the poetic distinction Bergamín employs between air, 'aire', and wind, 'viento'. Air seems to denote the divine and wind the human. However, the distinction only functions on the denotative level since the connotative inferences one might be tempted to draw upon for each image cover the same semantic territory. The metaphors work on the basis of a false polarization. Their combined attempt to avoid the self-annihilating implications of the paradoxical utterance has, nevertheless, condemned their metaphorical value to an expression of Man's linguistic and intellectual incompetence.   The difference of degree on an immeasurable yardstick destroys Man's projections of the Other by condemning language to an inescapable self-reflexivity.

Human truth is depicted as a monstrous perversion of divine perfection; a disastrous and painful approximation:

> La verdad es que la vida
> no es una línea derecha   ·
> sino una línea torcida.
>
> Preso en su laberinto
> el corazón es un monstruo
> que se devora a sí mismo.
>
> (*Poesía, IV*, p. 52)

The image is of the monstrous dilemma created by misplaced logic in an illogical world, a world which nevertheless necessitates the use of such an ordering principle.   Reason is doomed from the start by the fundamental disparity between Man's will to live and the inevitability of his demise: Man is trying to explain the inexplicable and the unacceptable. Bergamín does not even trust any sensual proof of his existence; any physical presence is challenged by the unanswerable nature of Man's inability to discern a real difference between Being and Non-being, precisely because of the terrifying unknowability of death:

> ¡Ay! siento que mi vida es como si no fuera
> mi vida, sino otra, de apagada ilusión.
>
> (*Poesía, II*, p. 72)

Personality, individual identity, is a meaningless concept when not even paradoxes can be circumscribed: life is not life, but it is not death either, rather another life, which although more conceivable than death, is still sensually and intellectually out of reach, indefinite. Bergamín can do no more than glimpse possibilities and hope for the arbitrary gift of faith in a fixed, divine order:

> La imagen que refleja esa profunda
> oquedad de misterio
> se apaga poco a poco a los sentidos
> como se apaga un eco.

(Poesía, II, p. 74)

Curiously enough, the most affirmative expression of faith in life and utterance is Bergamín's insistence upon its continual loss, the incessant depletion of any sense of meaning. Loss suggests a past of possible possession of faith, or surety, or validity of utterance:

> Yo sentía esta noche
> cuando estaba dormido
> latir mi corazón
> de otro modo distinto:
>
> como si, de repente,
> alterase su ritmo
> y, poco a poco, fuese
> cesando en su latido.

(Poesía, II, p. 52)

And also:

> El reloj dando las horas
> no nos las da, nos las quita:
> nos roba el tiempo, robándonos
> con él, el alma y la vida.

(Poesía, II, p. 34)

If one turns briefly to Bergamín´s seminal essay 'La importancia del demonio', his convictions about the insufficiency of material existence and the incapacity of human intellectual and sensual faculties become more comprehensible once viewed from within the parameters of his religious sensibility. In the essay, he portrays a mythical landscape which describes, in the first place, the Greek vision of the universe where humanity is separated from the gods by the demonic realm. The demon of the air could, according to the Greeks, act as a divine intercessor or mediator:

La diferencia entre estos mundos era una distinción o distancia sencillamente elemental: el mundo elemental de los hombres es la tierra; el de los dioses, el cielo etéreo; el de los demonios, el aire. [...] Esta naturaleza aérea o airada del Demonio, o de los demonios, tenía, para los griegos, el sentido de intercesión o mediación divina.[20]

According to Christian doctrine, however, this quintessentially hermetic demon is a false mediator, a monstrous opposite to Christ:

El mito de Hermes sintetiza todas las cualidades demoníacas intermedias entre los hombres y los dioses; por esto en el Hermes griego como en su equivalente latino Mercurio, vieron los cristianos una perfecta representación o encarnación idólatra del Demonio. Por ser ésta, su naturaleza demoníaca de mediador divino, la causa por la cual más finamente se le acusa en el cristianismo cuando con las palabras de San Pablo se afirmaba que el único medianero de Dios y de los hombres es Cristo Jesús. (p. 106)

The Christian interpretation of the spiritual landscape differs from the Greek in that the demons of air and light were, for the Christian, willingly or wilfully separated from God:

No cabe, pues, para el cristiano mediación celeste; ni aun, en este sentido, de los ángeles. Por eso el cristianismo nos ofrece de esta plenitud espiritual del universo otra interpretación distinta: todas las criaturas celestes (dioses y demonios de los griegos) de idéntica naturaleza elemental, no solamente aérea, sino luminosa, fueron, en una tercera parte, separadas de Dios; y no por su propia naturaleza, como dice San Agustín, sino por su propia voluntad. (p. 107)

Although by inhabiting a demonic world, Man is blind to the reality of God, he is usually deluded into thinking that his perceptions are complete because the devil's spirit fuses into the medium of those perceptions: the devil's natural place is the air and the light: 'Pero habría que advertir que esa sombra de lo divino puede aparecer a nuestros sentidos como luz. El Demonio puede ser para nosotros luz' (p. 107). Thus air and light are the masks of a hidden reality; for Bergamín the material world is an anti-reality:

El que nace todas las mañanas, según las palabras proféticas, es, para nosotros, el Demonio; su luz es nuestra luz: la sombra divina; lo cual, aunque parezca irónico, sería como decir que lo que denominamos nuestro sistema solar, materialmente es el sistema mismo del Demonio. (p. 108)

And language too, hermetic in nature, suffers the same ineffectual fate because the divine nature of music and the word is marked by the devil rather than by God; language masks the reality of God:

A Hermes se atribuye también en su mito la invención de la música y de la palabra. Hermes quiere decir eso mismo: la palabra celeste. La palabra y la música que son por el aire. Hermes, divinidad, o dios del aire o de los aires, es como una personificación de todos los demonios; y viene así a presentársenos como un anti-Cristo, que es, en definitiva, como un anti-Dios o contra-Dios: como demonio de los demonios, como el mismísimo Demonio. (pp. 107-08)

Even though such a vision appears to condemn Man to a permanent state of delusion, this is evidently not the case, given that Bergamín can perceive the illusory nature of the world. In fact he is at pains to point out that it is only

materiality which is so obscenely constrained into the demonic perspective and
that it is important to become aware of the partiality of this perspective:

Este punto de vista es precisamente el punto de vista del Demonio. [...] Pero digo que no
hay que alarmarse por ello, porque de afirmar que el Demonio tenga importancia a creer
que sea el único que tiene verdadera importancia hay un abismo, que es el suyo, el de su
caída, el de su infierno, el de su propia naturaleza abismática. Por eso, si no hay que
quitarle al Demonio toda su importancia, tampoco hay que darle demasiada, que es lo que
ha hecho siempre, y se llama como se llame en la Historia todo materialismo, todo punto de
vista exclusivamente materialista, que es el punto de vista propio del Demonio. (p. 109)

The material world, the demonic realm, is characterized by the absence of
God; the world is a world of estrangement from God:

En esta teoría, la ausencia de Dios es la concentración de la luz divina en sí misma. Es que
Dios se vuelve de espaldas a lo creado y proyecta sobre nosotros esa luz tenebrosa de su
sombra, y entonces el mundo se convierte en el imperio infernal, sombríamente luminoso,
de la materia, que es el imperio mismo del Demonio. Por eso dice San Juan en su
Evangelio que Cristo ha vencido al mundo cuando vence al Demonio. (p. 109)

This demonic world, of course, is the incarnation of what God is not, not life
but death:

El Demonio es, como San Agustín lo definía, no un no ser, no nada, sino una voluntad de
no ser, una voluntad de la nada; [...] Todo lo contrario que Dios. (p. 110)

This is why Bergamín portrays his poetic landscape as a world permeated by
the continual presence of death, the 'voluntad totalizadora del no ser' (p. 110):

'Como angélica criatura capaz de todas las ciencias', según nos dice en un admirable verso
Calderón, tenía el Demonio que inmortalizarse en su caída: perpetuándose en un infinito
afán perecedero, en esa absorción espiritual abismática; por esa vertiginosa precipitación en
su abismo, en el que vive o muere cayendo, porque es una especie de muerte inmortal la
suya: como la de la música por el sonido o la de la palabra por la voz. (pp. 109-10)

The devil's task is to lead Man away from God, towards death:

Por eso su voluntad nos lleva a la muerte definitiva, que es su infierno. Por eso nos trae y
nos lleva, herméticamente, guiándonos, para perdernos mejor, para quitarnos el sentido
divino de la vida, [...] Para hacernos perder el único sentido verdadero de la vida: el de
Dios. (p. 111)

Consequently, life as it is experienced in the material world is an illusion of
life. It is, paradoxically, a deathly state:

La más aguda y penetrante definición poética de la muerte que conozco es la que nos dejó Heráclito al decir que la muerte es lo que sentimos cuando estamos despiertos. (p. 113)

Bergamín's representation of the human condition within the mythical parameters of his religious vision underpins his poetic portrayal of Being. He describes the world as a place of shades, torment, and death exiled from God:

Sentimos nuestra vida porque estamos despiertos y en esa vigilancia de la vida sentimos la muerte: sentimos al Demonio, que es la voluntad de la muerte; porque no podíamos sentir la muerte sino como una voluntad contraria a Dios, contraria a la vida: como voluntad del Demonio. (pp. 113-14)

His poetry speaks of the dislocation that the material, demonic world inspires. Since the devil colours human perception with his 'voluntad contraria a Dios', our perceptions denote separation from, rather than unity with, God. Bergamín's conviction is that life constitutes an agony of the awareness of separation, a separateness which deludes us into investing in this separateness:

Y es esta voluntad la que tocándonos en lo que sentimos, y en lo que más sentimos, la que dividiendo nuestro común sentir, nos precisa y apura toda la vida en sensaciones separadas: para engañarnos. (p. 114)

Bergamín's mockery of differences without distinction reveals his scorn of the demonic world and his desire to rediscover a totalizing vision of transcendence rather than to succumb to the confusion of the divisive definitions that were instigated in the Fall:

El Demonio divide, para vencernos, nuestro total sentido humano de la vida en muchos otros: lo divide en todos sentidos; y en cada uno de estos sentidos, nos tienta: esto es, que nos toca perceptible o imperceptiblemente, para confundirnos: para confundir nuestra percepción natural y sobrenatural del mundo. Por eso, la percepción del mundo que tenemos por nuestros sentidos, desde la caída de Adán, es una percepción confusa: una percepción del Demonio. (p. 114)

The oneness of God is counterposed to the multiplicity of the devil: 'Es esta multiplicidad del ser unida por la sombra, la que nos da una idea del Demonio' (p. 115). This denomination alone explains the difficulty Bergamín experiences with the notion of identity. Identity in the world denotes a separation and, at its most demonic, a multiplicity which insults the notion of oneness with God, of true identity with God in a transcendent realm which exists beyond all definition, beyond the material world: 'La soledad del hombre sin Dios — que quería Nietzsche — no es otra cosa que el Demonio' (p. 119). The imperative of Bergamín's dialectics of faith arises from the need to cast into doubt the supposedly certain, material demonic world and uncover its illusory, deathly nature:

La muerte es lo cierto: la vida es lo incierto, lo dudoso: la inmortalidad — dije alguna vez —. Habrá, pues, que dejar siempre lo cierto por lo dudoso. Dejar lo cierto por lo dudoso es dejar la muerte por la vida, es dejar al Demonio por Dios: cambiar, en definitiva, la certeza por la fe. (p. 117)

THE DEVIL'S ADVOCATE

The mythical portrayal of the absence of God, which is the world, as the constitution of another divine figure, that of the devil, is not merely picturesque; it is essential to Bergamín's dialectics of faith. Both God and the devil are divine in nature. If this were not the case Man would not be conscious of his predicament, would not be aware of the Fall from grace. The material world, because it is divine, although divinely mortal, partakes of the divine imagination. The two-sided nature of the devil (he is both heavenly and earthly) provides Man with a glimpse of salvation, and the material world is the site of the battle in Man's imagination between God and the Devil. The dialectics of faith necessitates the instability and continual movement of a process of 'desengaño', which reveals a potential for human transcendence. The clash of two divine spirits constitutes a vital spark:

Esta luz material en que vivimos o de que vivimos no es otra cosa que como un chispazo, un corto circuito celeste: un contacto cósmico de la voluntad positiva de Dios con la negativa del Demonio. (p. 108)

For this reason, the material world cannot be totally rejected in favour of a spiritual reality beyond the material. The material world, and most significantly the body as the house of the soul, provides the context for salvation and cannot be denied in human terms: hence the doctrinal necessity of the resurrection of the flesh. So the material world, despite its material masquerading, provides the key to transcendence. The dialectics of faith is a continual reinvestment in the imagination and the body and the contemplation of the material unmasks not only the deathly potential of Man but also its opposite, the transcendent desire of Man.

The conflation of opposites I have been sketching is perhaps best illustrated in Bergamín's depiction of women. Woman as the earthly essence of otherness circumscribes the field of struggle for identity for Bergamín. This identity on the one hand requires separation in order to persist in the material world and yet, on the other hand, yearns for communion with otherness and the destruction of the constraining definitions of that material existence, which, in other words, yearns for the sublime.

Bergamín's portrayal of woman is understandably volatile, changing, transmuting from glimpses of divine potential to visions of darkness and isolation. The figures of women, and the figuring of Bergamín's desire for love and communication, reveal the way Logos gains and loses credence; how continual change and displacement of perspective combat the thought that Logos may not provide a divine yardstick; how a combative and accusatory stance forces language to redefine itself from moment to moment to encompass infinite shades of potential.

Woman, for Bergamín, is the incarnation of the Other and an image of death, the latter deriving from literary ideas of courtly love, from Petrarch and Quevedo.   Woman is an objectification, a reification, of the relationship between Self and otherness for Bergamín; she has no existence apart from his articulation of her and yet he feels shut out from her sphere of reference.   In Lacanian terms, Woman as the Other is the 'locus of the constitution of the subject or the structure that produces the subject'.[21] This would be enough for Lacan but is a mixed blessing for Bergamín, for definition as a subject in the world carries with it the correspondent implication for Bergamín that such subjectivity is paid for with death.   Woman is the image of language and the sum of the implications of death; Woman is metaphor.   She enacts through Bergamín the ambiguities and complexities of his views by embodying, at least mythically, the ephemerality, insubstantiality, generality, and unanswerable indistinctness of any concept of life, reality, God, and death.   She is a multiplicity of realities and above all, she is deathly, untouchable but physically undeniable, and eternally out of reach:

> Tú eres como la muerte
> que cuando va llegando
> al corazón, parece
> que detiene sus pasos.
>
> Como si no quisiera
> apagar con su mano
> de nieve, el fuego vivo
> que nos está quemando.

(*Poesía, IV*, p. 20)

Woman becomes the object of mystical depictions of Logos, of the void; she is both diabolical and divine:

> Tú eres abismo,
> sima sin fondo,

> alma de cántaro,
> hueco sonoro:
>
> del espantable
> vacío de todo
> eres el eco
> más tenebroso;
>
> no eres la máscara
> de ningún rostro:
> eres sombrío
> disfraz diabólico.

(Poesía, IV, p. 19)

And her opacity, her impenetrability is synonymous with the void:

> Debías llamarte oscura
> en vez de llamarte Clara
> porque hasta la luz se vuelve
> tenebrosa en tu mirada.
>
> Oscuro es tu corazón,
> oscuras son tus palabras,
> es oscuro lo que piensas,
> lo que sientes, lo que hablas.
>
> Y es tanta la oscuridad
> de la noche de tu alma
> que se apagan en tus ojos
> las estrellas solitarias.

(Poesía, IV, p. 16)

Infinitely distressing, she is also infinitely desirable; her 'ansiedad de infinitudes' is reminiscent of the Lacanian notion that death signifies the ultimate consummation of all desire.[22] Occasionally Bergamín will articulate the fluidity that informs the reflexivity of the Woman and the void. For Woman does not answer the imperatives to justify her existence and does not comply with the poet's demands for communication. She is both light and darkness, refusing particularization as well as absolute generalization:

> No sé si son tus ojos
> los que al mirarme ahora
> la luz del sol de pronto
> me vuelven tenebrosa:
>
> como si de su llama
> me volviesen la sombra

> hundiéndome en la sima
> infernal de su aurora.

(Poesía, IV, p. 32)

Bergamín is far less able to negate definitively than he is to affirm. He may continually affirm absence but, paradoxically, he cannot deny presence. Although in real terms this distinction seems tautologous, false even, Bergamín does see a difference between the actions of affirmation and negation of absence and presence (and vice-versa) even though the end result appears to be the same. In fact, such apparent sameness continually frustrates Bergamín and adds a tragic mockery to his poetic voice. In the previous poem he uses the language of doubt, 'no sé' and 'como si'. There is a linguistic gap here which implies a potential to regain shifting or lost meaning. For instance, amidst his love poems (more accurately, meanderings around the concept of utterance) he sometimes forsakes his projections of Woman, the muse, the external that defines his internal reality/illusion and admits or rather affirms the Self as his only constant, although of course even that is mutable and unstable. He describes the fear that such responsibility provokes in him:

> Todo lo que escucho,
> todo lo que miro,
> es eco y es sombra
> fugaz de mí mismo:
>
> en la tenebrosa
> noche del sentido
> todo es espantable
> silencio infinito.

(Poesía, IV, p. 21)

In this poem, Bergamín leaps from the particular to the general, from the human to the divine (from the first stanza to the second), creating a haiku-like juxtaposition of subject and object, the individual against the world, the void, the silence. The harmony of the juxtaposition seems absolute, invoking a potential resolution of philosophical paradox through language, ironically the tool of thought. This expression of paradox in the poem, however, denotes an idea of the absolute or of completeness versus Man, the partial, the fragment, the particular as resolvable, which is seemingly contradicted at the same time by the very image Bergamín uses to depict such a totality: 'todo es eco y es sombra'. Only this visual image of insubstantiality succeeds in maintaining the subtlety of Bergamín's intellectual integrity: the central colon in the poem tears open the assumption of harmony, acting as the pivot for Logos, designating an unutterable centre or yardstick of expression. The colon creates a linguistic gap, an absence, or rather delay, which, whilst displacing utterance, creates meaning, creates the suspicion that harmony is illusory and causes the reader to concentrate on the redoubled doubt of the fugitive shade, the echoed voice of Self that laughably seeks to contend with Infinity.

Similarly with the image of Woman, Bergamín admits that his vision is flawed. Love, though at times all-consuming and positive, is, even so, marked by the absence of action or of any positive articulation on the part of the women Bergamín speaks of and to. Bergamín waits in vain for a fixable, verifiable response:

> Yo estoy esperando siempre
> ver clarear la mañana
> con otra luz y con otros ojos
> en los que pueda mirarla;

(Poesía, II, p. 77)

And:

> Que, al fin, lo que te queda de la vida
> es sentir el vacío de otra mano
> en tu mano vacía.

(Poesía, II, p. 66)

And in Woman, when she does respond, Bergamín identifies a similar discrepancy between words and their meaning, a discrepancy which, although negative, holds a potential affirmation: meaning slippage denoting a possible meaning gain. Somewhere between the sound of her voice and the words she utters lies the essence that is forever out of reach:

> Temeroso de los silencios
> tu voz parece, cuando callas,
> alejarse de la espesura
> tenebrosa de las palabras.

(Poesía, II, p. 58)

If nothing else, he sets himself the task of describing his alienation from the world of Woman and his frustration at the solipsistic and futile nature of communication:

> Tú en tu sueño. Yo en mi sueño.
> Entre los dos corre el río
> oscuro del pensamiento.
>
> De un pensamiento huidero
> de sí mismo que no sabe
> siquiera de qué va huyendo.   *(Poesía, IV*, p. 36)

FRONTERAS INFERNALES DE LA POESÍA

Certainly Bergamín saw poetry as an accusatory or at least oppositional discourse. Is poetry the language of the gods? At least Bergamín attempts to exploit the difference between poetry or Art and the more mundane, or particularized types of writing, representing it as a language apart which, by dint of its separateness, operates within a closed frame of reference, a mythic reference, which can thereby attempt to mirror the complexities and ambiguities of Man's stance in relation to Logos. Central to his aesthetic ideas is this oppositional questioning of the reality of, and his challenge to the meaning of death, through poetry:

El poeta se pregunta a sí mismo por la muerte, y pregunta a la muerte por sí mismo, por su propio destino. La poesía por fronteriza de la muerte es la que puede contestar a estas preguntas.[23]

Not only does poetry challenge the defining contours of consciousness, poetic discourse in Bergamín's terms becomes a challenging centre of Logos which attempts to displace death as the unknown essence of discourse. Death and poetry and their oxymoronic definitions become interchangeable and interdependent: where death defines poetry, poetry defines death:

Trazando la naturaleza y figuración fronteriza de la poesía, encontramos, en sus fronteras, una sola letra inicial por las que todas sus definiciones nominales comienzan: letra inicial que es la de la muerte. (p. 9)

'La poesía pregunta por la muerte', and is also, by virtue of their relationship, 'la que puede contestar a estas preguntas: ¿dónde está el Infierno? ¿más allá o más acá de la muerte?' (pp. 9-10). Poetry must turn in upon itself, work within its own metaphysics, but become also an identifiable artefact of itself. Bergamín exploits the double connotation of 'ensimismamiento' and 'en sí mismo' to imbue poetry with a self-sufficiency and potential for paring down to essentials that allows it to approximate to Truth:

Cuando la poesía vuelve sobre sí misma su propio sentir y sentido, cuando *se ensimisma*, se concentra, definiéndose, delimitándose, trazando sus fronteras, por su propia magia o metafísica, mística, moral o música, que la encierra en círculos concéntricos definidores de ese ensimismamiento, [...] Dentro o fuera del hombre, esa [la muerte] es la línea definidora de la poesía. (p. 9)

According to Bergamín, poetic language has a similar task to that of identity; that of dissolving the definitions that condemn it to a deathly nature. Just as the image of Woman encapsulates the demonic (she is both heavenly and earthly), so too poetic language reveals a two-sided divine nature which, paradoxically, inheres in the material artefact of the poem in the same way as Woman resides most definitively in the flesh.[24]

The notion of the artefact of poetry is extrapolated in 'El pensamiento hermético de las artes', an essay which exploits the image of a coin to describe the dualities, the binary oppositional forces in poetic language which operate in the creative dynamic:[25] 'En las nuevas artes poéticas, la razón se diviniza con dos caras, como una moneda: una órfica y otra hermética' (p. 43). Again, it is the divine nature of the devil which provides the possibility of a vision which is not fatally contaminated with mortality; the materiality that poetic language aspires to is divine rather than human and so escapes the curse of degeneration: 'Las artes poéticas de hacer cosas de juego, cosas de razón, son verdaderas porque son divinas, y a la inversa; según del lado que se mire la misma moneda' (p. 44).

The salvationary potential of poetry, founded on the tension between its dual process, a journey towards and a journey away from Hell, derives from the double-edged demonic nature of poetic discourse itself: 'El doble sentido del pensar poético, del pensamiento poéticamente puro o recién nacido inmortal a que los griegos llamaron Hermes' (p. 45). Poetry, then, is a privileged discourse for Bergamín, a dialectical process of continual rebirth:

La razón de ser de todas las artes poéticas es este pensamiento recién nacido de la razón divina: este pensamiento puro; y por eso son nuevas las artes: porque son poéticas, porque acaban, siempre, herméticamente de nacer. (p. 45)

And, naturally, true poetic discourse is one which rejects the constraints of History: 'Y es que para llegar a la veracidad poética hay que eliminar absolutamente la Historia y con ella ese aspecto vital de sus perspectivas como criterio de valoración' (pp. 48-49).

Of course, the vitalistic vision of Man, being as it is his natural state of estrangement from God, leaves the poetic persona in an appalling predicament, in a prisonhouse of language and experience. Bergamín's description of 'true' poetic discourse in 'El pensamiento hermético de las artes' is a utopian vision to which he can only rarely aspire in his poetry. The language of modernity, as I have already suggested, militates against the notion of transcendence and often the hegemony of the material world shapes an anguished, albeit necessarily anguished, stance in the face of a vital experience which is apparently condemned to a conceptual and linguistic binary trap, dictated by the deathly discourse of mortality.

Although loss or gain of meaning by affirmation or negation sets up a dialectical process of signification, a promise at least of some sort of expressivity, Bergamín is simultaneously faced with not only the uncertainties enacted in such binary affirmations and negations, but also with the agonizing question of the validity of such binarism in the first place. Escaping from a two-dimensional concept of language in order to encompass the divine seems to entail the destruction of the very concept of the divine itself, a thought which provokes a desperate, hollow hopelessness in the poetic persona:

> ¿quién mató a Dios, qué mano tenebrosa
> lo sepultó en su sueño?
>
> *(Poesía, VII,* p. 54)

Bergamín at times even surrenders to a derisively ambivalent attitude to such questioning and soul-searching. After all, what difference does it make?:

> Si todo lo que es, fuese tan solo
> apariencia de serlo,
> el alma seguiría siendo el alma
> y el sueño siendo el sueño.
>
> *(Poesía, IV,* p. 59)

At times, Bergamín appears tired of life and almost yearns for death:

> ¡Ay perezosa y larga
> muerte! ¿Por qué no vienes
> a llevarme contigo
> de una vez para siempre?
>
> *(Poesía, IV,* p. 22)

He is, however, ultimately convinced of a moral imperative to keep searching for surety. He does not definitively doubt the existence of order, he simply doubts Man's ability to conceive of it. This becomes a moral issue, a moral imperative, a search for life in death, for the divine in the human:

> La luz nace de la sombra
> y por la sombra se muere.
> Nadie se encuentra a sí mismo
> si primero no se pierde.
>
> *(Poesía, VII,* p. 34)

Bergamín doubts the oxymoronic nature of reality; in his logocentrism 'los extremos se tocan':

> Nunca el fuego luminoso
> en su llama se levanta
> tanto, como cuando cae
> con sus sombras en la nada.
>
> *(Poesía, VII,* p. 78)

He questions his particular human existence or, more exactly, his perceptual capacity to distinguish between the life of the body and the spirit, and ultimately to pinpoint the fallacious illusions of reality and their inevitably false depictions in language:

> No sé siquiera dónde tengo el cuerpo
> ni dónde está mi alma.
> Y apenas si una llama mortecina
> agoniza en mi lámpara.
>
> *(Poesía, VII, p. 72)*

His identity is dislocated from his logocentrism, a belief in God and the Word is not necessarily an assurance of personal existence. Bergamín is not contained within his own vision; his vision is of an absence, an absence of God. He tries, therefore, to absent himself in order to define himself as present: the objectivization of the Subject, of himself, becomes a tangled mass of perceptions, none of which has any divine yardstick, despite the 'presencia viva de la muerte':

> Porque pienso que no pienso
> siento que me estoy pensando
> fuera de mi pensamiento.
>
> Como si estuviera muerto
> y me sintiera dormir
> por debajo de mi sueño.
>
> *(Poesía, IV, p. 28)*

Shades of meaning about Being and Non-being can only validate themselves in relation to themselves, and the continual displacement of these shades of meaning provides the only glimpses of Logos, of true utterance. Landscapes of dream, sleep, and air are so intangible as to provoke an angst in Bergamín which far exceeds his original angst about death: even death now is irrelevant when he is faced with the illusion of illusions of his own utterance:

> O es un fantasmal sonido
> como el oscuro latir
> del corazón en mi oído.
>
> *(Poesía, IV, p. 30)*

And also:

> Yo estoy diciendo palabras,
> palabras sin voz ni eco,
> palabras que yo no sé
> por qué las estoy diciendo.

Son palabras sin sonido,
palabras sin pensamiento,
que vosotros no entendéis
y que yo tampoco entiendo.

Palabras mudas que son
mensajeras del silencio:
palabras que oyen tan sólo
los que escuchan a los muertos.

(Poesía, VII, p. 71)

The landscape of the soul, though, does not cease to exist. It is described over and over again, but it is a deserted landscape:

Yo tenía un alma viva
que se reía en mis huesos.
Ahora mi alma está muerta
y está roto mi esqueleto.

(Poesía, VII, p. 73)

Perhaps the most disturbing thing about Bergamín's philosophical and linguistic anguish is his refusal to reject words such as 'alma', 'espíritu', or 'infinito'. His desperate reapproximation of them is born of the fixity of dualities which, although rejected by him, he is condemned to pander to as his only, though flawed, line of reasoning. 'La letra inicial de la muerte' remains a constant and gruelling preoccupation, the hangman's arm and a life-saving rope, an insistent recommendation for Alpha and Omega: if there is an end, then perhaps there is a beginning; an echo, so a voice; a silence that terrifies and a 'soledad sonora'. It is as if as long as the words exist, then the ideas cannot be obsolete, or can they?:

Soy como el eco que a tu voz responde,
como la sombra que a tu cuerpo sigue,
como el espejo que a tu rostro esconde.

Soy como el parecer que al ser convierte
en aparente sueño de la vida,
espejo, sombra y eco de la muerte.

(Poesía, I, p. 88)

It is only through a contemplation of the material, bodily nature of language that Bergamín is to be able to reinvest the language of transcendence with validity. In the following chapter I shall examine how the body, as the only, though constantly diminishing, reality we know challenges its own mortal state by destabilizing its rational context. Poetic discourse is potentially an anti-rational discourse for Bergamín, one which through a paradoxical investment in its bodily nature attempts to transcend the constraints of material reality in the world and re-identify the body with the spirit, the finite with the infinite, and the human with the divine according to the dialectics of faith, the movement of which constitutes a persistent realignment of our perceptions and our language to the transcendent realm of the divine. For Bergamín this process is a Christian process, the Word made Flesh in Christ and the Flesh resurrected in the image of divinity through the paradoxical mortification of its material reality. In his poetry the process of restitution is articulated as continual rebirth, a trope which unites both Bergamín´s religious reading of the human condition and his conceptual representation of the functioning of language in poetic discourse.

NOTES

1 Broadly speaking, Bergamín's notions of 'hermetic' and 'Orphic' poetic language coincide with those elucidated by Gerald L. Bruns in his *Modern Poetry and the Idea of Language* (New Haven, CT: Yale University Press, 1974), namely that: 'We can call the first idea "hermetic", because the direction of the poet's activity is toward the literary work as such, that is, the work as a self-contained linguistic structure. [...] We can call the second idea "Orphic", after Orpheus, the primordial singer whose sphere of activity is governed by a mythical or ideal unity of word and being, and whose power extends therefore beyond the formation of a work toward the creation of the world' (p. 1).

2 Julia Kristeva, 'On the Melancholic Imaginary', in *Discourse in Psychoanalysis and Literature*, pp. 109-10.

3 Nigel Dennis, 'José Bergamín (1895-1983)', *Insula*, no. 443, (October 1983), 3.

4 *Cruz y Raya: Revista de afirmación y negación* (Madrid: Cruz y Raya, 1933-36), 15 April 1933, 7-10 (p.10).

5 Nigel Dennis, *El aposento en el aire: Introducción a la poesía de José Bergamín*, p. 23.

6 *Cruz y Raya*, 15 April 1933, p. 9.

7 José Bergamín, *Poesía, I: Sonetos, Rimas, Del otoño y los mirlos* (Madrid: Turner, 1983), p. 92.

8 José Bergamín, *El cohete y la estrella/La cabeza a pájaros*, pp. 93, 94.

9 See Nigel Dennis, 'Unamuno and Bergamín: Contexts of a Correspondence', *Revista Canadiense de Estudios Hispánicos*, 11 (1987), 257-87.

10 *Cruz y Raya*, 15 April 1933, p. 10.

11 José Bergamín, *Poesía, IV: Velado desvelo (1973-1977)* (Madrid: Turner, 1983), p. 53.

12 Miguel de Unamuno, *Del sentimiento trágico de la vida*, p. 31.

13 Miguel de Unamuno, *La agonía del cristianismo*, p. 39.

14 José Bergamín, *Poesía, III: Apartada orilla (1971-1972)* (Madrid: Turner, 1983), p. 67.

15 Nigel Dennis, 'José Bergamín y su "clavo ardiendo"', *Insula*, no. 341 (April 1975), 1, 13 (p.13).

16 Ramón Gaya, 'Epilogue pour un livre', in Delay and Letournier, pp. 265-72 (p. 265).

17 José Bergamín, *Poesía, VII: Hora última* (Madrid: Turner, 1984), p. 56.

18 *Cruz y Raya*, 15 April 1933, 41-66.

19 José Bergamín, *Poesía, II: La claridad desierta* (Madrid: Turner, 1983), p. 62.

20 José Bergamín, 'La importancia del demonio', in *La importancia del demonio y otras cosas sin importancia* (Madrid: Júcar, 1974), pp. 103-33 (p. 105).

21 Toril Moi, *Sexual/Textual Politics: Feminist Literary Theory* (London and New York: Methuen , 1985), p. 101.

22 Lacan draws on the ideas of Freud in connecting sexual satiation with death. See especially Sigmund Freud, 'Beyond the Pleasure Principle', in Sigmund Freud, *The Essentials of Psycho-Analysis* (London: Hogarth Press and the Institute of Psycho-analysis, 1986), pp. 218-67.

[23] *Fronteras infernales de la poesía*, pp. 9-10.

[24] I use the word 'demonic' advisedly here. I am not referring to the demoniacal or diabolical nature of Woman although, as we have seen, Bergamín does at times see her in such a negative light. Rather, I am referring to the potential of Woman to embody both human mortality and divine potential, the fusion of which, for the poet, reflects the 'demonic' state of the world.

[25] See footnote 1 of this chapter for an explanation of 'hermetic' and 'Orphic' poetic language.

CHAPTER 4

CHRISTIANITY

THE BODY

Christianity for Bergamín tries to reconcile a discrepancy between the body
and the soul. As I have already outlined, Bergamín sees the material world as
demonic, full of masks, as is language. He rejects the static nature of those
masks in favour of a continual movement away from the fixed forms of
rationality. For him, life and art are a continual sacrament. Sacrament
involves the capturing , killing, and consumption of reality as it is given to us,
in order to purify and create a new vision. This is a fluid, continually moving,
wandering vision for Bergamín. The figure of Christ is the classic sacrament,
the killing of the body in order to free the spirit, the denial of material reality in
favour of transcendent reality, promoting eventually the resurrection of the
flesh. For Bergamín this can only happen with the admittance of the feminine.
In the 'Tres sonetos a Cristo crucificado ante el mar' this is the sea, the
generative principle of eternal life, cyclical and fluid.

In the previous chapter I examined how the demonic nature of the material
world is both divine and human for Bergamín: it is thus both potentially
transcendent and apparently deathly. It is through the bodily as well as the
transcendent nature of reality and language that Bergamín hopes to validate his
Christian language of transcendence. The body is not simply a vessel for the
soul, according to Bergamín; the body is consubstantial with the soul:

> No tenemos alma:
> tenemos un cuerpo que encarna el espíritu
> y lo desencarna.
>
> En una palabra,
> somos la palabra resucitadora
> de un Dios que se calla.
>
> De un Dios que no habla
> y que nos la calla con tanto silencio
> que hay que adivinarla.

Que hay que figuarársela
como si no fuésemos nosotros la sombra
de su llama viva.

(*Poesías casi completas*, p. 165)

Humanity, then, contributes to the creation of a vision of divinity. The bodily, material nature of man is the source of the rupturing of divine opacity and silence. Paradoxically, mortality and materiality are the instigators of divine expression, of the 'palabra resucitadora/ de un Dios que se calla'.

The body constrained to temporality constitutes its conceptual contrary: the soul, ineffable and eternal. Bergamín extrapolates the idea that time and the soul are one and the same in *El clavo ardiendo*. The body and the soul are as inter-related as time and space and, in addition, the body inevitably exists in time, and time has a material nature. Indeed, the materiality of time is construed as soul, or at least an affirmation of the soul, given that Bergamín's vision of life on this earth is of a life with a purpose, that of achieving eternal life for the material as well as the spiritual:

'El espacio traspasa el tiempo como el cuerpo el alma', escribe Novalis. 'Si no hubiera alma no habría tiempo', repetían con San Agustín los escolásticos. También los poetas y pensadores modernos insisten en la romántica apreciación del tiempo como sustancia y no accidente, como esencial existencia y subsistencia posible de la poesía. Del tiempo que es alma: el *tiempo material*.[1]

Bergamín's vision of eternity is dependent upon the notion of linear, material time shot through with eternal moments, a dialectical, oscillating equilibrium, the shocks of linear time forging eternity:

Y, precisamente, la eternidad: la trasmutación temporal del 'momento histórico' en 'instante eterno'; un tornadizo balanceo, tras el que la mudanza, el cambio, se ha verificado, a su vez, instantáneamente, momentáneamente, como pasajero y eterno; no sólo tornándose en otro y el mismo, sino trastornándose de ese modo. (p. 113)

Ultimately, this reference to upheaval, 'trastorno', rupture even, in relation to the creation of eternity, becomes in religious terms a disruption akin to wounding as Bergamín develops his sacramental vision of Christ as the creator of eternal life through the mortification of His flesh:

El que se cristiana o cristianiza misteriosamente por el signo (sacramento) verificador de la palabra y el agua unidas (como el agua y la sangre que brotan del costado del Cristo muerto) es el que muere a lo humano en él y vive para Dios. (p. 87)

The Christian experience of reality is one of suspension between two opposing worlds, the temporal and the eternal, however these two worlds happen to coexist for Bergamín:

Por la revelación cristiana de San Juan — por el Apocalipsis — nos aparece el hombre — el conocimiento del hombre — situado entre dos abismos: el hombre se conoce a sí mismo de este modo, suspendido entre dos abismos inmortales: uno de luz, otro de sombra; el abismo del conocimiento divino y la sima del conocimiento satánico.[2]

The eternal is continually evoked by the temporal, and is also a product of the material world:

> La presencia invisible de otro mundo
> en éste, que ahora veo
> como una evocación alucinante,
> trastorna lo que siento:
>
> y equivoca mis ojos al mirarlo
> como equivoca un sueño
> con su profunda realidad ilusoria
> los éxtasis del tiempo.
>
> Un pasado, presente; y un presente
> que pasa a venidero,
> suspenden el momento fugitivo
> en un instante eterno.
>
> (*Poesías casi completas*, p. 164)

The trickery involved in the equivocal evocation, that is the claim that the poet can perceive eternity despite his acknowledgement of his illusory worldly perceptions, doubles back on Bergamín's original claim that we live in a world of masks which hide from us the reality of God.[3]   To this extent, his is an imagined eternity and the truth of his vision of eternity is unveiled poetically and in poetry as an act of faith, for such a truth defies reason:

Este entendimiento no es discursivo, racional, sino intuitivo, poético. [...] La razón se espanta; pero la verdad se manifiesta de ese modo, como contraria a ella y hasta incompatible con ella.[4]

And such a truth is also the purpose of poetry for Bergamín.   In his preface to *El clavo ardiendo* Malraux points out as much:

Pero Bergamín afirma que todo lo sagrado es poesía.   Que la poesía es una expresión indispensable de la fe.   El vínculo que establece entre la poesía y lo sagrado parece complejo, pero en realidad es simple: tanto la poesía como lo sagrado convierten el tiempo en eternidad. [...] Toda vida, dice, está hecha de momentos históricos cruzados de instantes eternos. Cual la poesía suprema, el sacramento une la vida a la eternidad, funde la vida en eternidad. (p. 10)

Here Malraux is speaking specifically of sacrament, a concept to which I shall return later on in this chapter; however for the moment I simply wish to point to a cluster of concepts which have repercussions for Bergamín's concern with materiality and the body. These concepts of time and eternity, movement and transformation, irrationality, poetry, and the consubstantiality of the body and the soul, convert what appears to be a deathly fate into the potential to transcend one's humanity, which is a natural human urge: 'Lo propio del hombre es deshumanizarse para poderse divinizar: la finalidad de lo humano es lo divino.' (*El clavo ardiendo*, p. 70)

Bergamín's point of departure is that the body is the only reality we know, so that even when he is trying to portray the distancing of his soul from himself he can only express such a dislocation in terms of the body, imagistically conflating the body and the soul:

> Mi alma se aleja de mí.
> También se aleja mi cuerpo.
> Como si se separasen
> los dos de mi pensamiento.
>
> Tanto me voy alejando
> de mí mismo, que me siento
> sin piel, sin sangre, sin vida,
> descarnado hasta los huesos.
>
> Sin piel, sin sangre, sin vida,
> descarnado hasta los huesos,
> 'siendo un esqueleto vivo
> siendo un animado muerto'.
>
> (*Poesías casi completas*, p. 158)

Like Octavio Paz, he sees the material reality of the body as possessing a double purpose: that of affirming and denying itself:

The body is imaginary, not because it lacks reality, but because it is the most real reality: an image that is palpable yet ever-changing, and doomed to disappear.[5]

The body is therefore the source of all symbols, the language of passion which only death can silence. Fear of death is the fear of the loss of the body, 'sin piel, sin sangre, sin vida/descarnado hasta los huesos'. Bergamín cannot deny the body in favour of the spirit, for the body shapes the soul and provides the conditions not only of human expression but also of divine utterance: 'Tenemos un cuerpo que encarna el espíritu [...] En una palabra/somos la palabra resucitadora/ de un Dios que se calla' (*Poesías casi completas*, p. 165).

For Bergamín, to dominate the body would be to suppress the images it emits when the body, material reality, is for him the site of his potential salvation. Language too, if it is to give credence to its dualistic demonic nature, must recognize its bodily source. In this, Bergamín again accords with Paz's views:

For the reality of the body is a shifting image pinned down by desire. If language is the most perfect form of communication, the perfection of language cannot help but be erotic, and it includes death and silence: the failure of language ... Failure? Silence is not a failure, but the end result, the culmination of language. Why do we keep saying that death is absurd? What do we know about death? (p. 14)

In the case of Bergamín we shall come to see this language born of desire as the discourse created by the Fall, a knowledge of the flesh that brings about the knowledge of death, the language of lamentation, and the desire for transcendence.

Octavio Paz couches his vision of our dual reality in terms of the opposing forces of the reality and the pleasure principle, terms of reference which translate neatly into Bergamín's mortality/transcendence dichotomy. For Paz, as for Bergamín, poetic metaphor has bodily potential because it expresses our dual reality, the necessity of death and the wish to overcome it. Particularly interesting is Paz's insistence that art seeks to incarnate the body:

I do not deny that art, like everything we do, is sublimation, culture, an homage to death. But it is a sublimation that seeks to incarnate: to return to the body. [...] Art is the opposite of dissipation, in the physical and spiritual sense of the word: it is concentration, desire that seeks incarnation. (p. 15)

For Bergamín, as for Paz, mortality is a linguistic problem. Bergamín's insistence on language's material, temporal nature, its deathly nature, places language firmly in the bodily realm. Indeed, as Bergamín observes in *El clavo ardiendo*, sacred language and the language of poetry are mediated through the senses:

La imagen o imágenes sensibles del lenguaje sacramental se nos hacen inteligibles por la sensibilización de este lenguaje para los ojos y los oídos; y al hacérsenos inteligible su representación misteriosa (sacramental) afecta, ante todo, a los sentidos, y su verificación por ellos es primordial para su entendimiento. (p. 39)

And poetic language challenges its own mortal state by destabilizing its rational context, by seeking in the body not the rationality of mortality but the irrationality of eternal life, a constant process of renewal, through sacrament, and ultimately in a Christian context through the sacrifice and resurrection of the body:

> Convertir un 'momento histórico' en un 'instante eterno' es lo que hace, decíamos, la poesía. Y es lo que poéticamente, claro es, hace el sacramento de la penitencia. Una vez más, comprobamos cómo la verificación sacramental lleva consigo, ineludiblemente, inseparablemente unida, su expresión poética. (pp. 99-100)

Any expression of faith, according to Bergamín, is necessarily poetic because only poetic discourse can partake of divinity:

> Por lo que diríamos, como aclaración a lo que venimos diciendo, que la poesía puede separarse de la fe y de sus expresiones religiosas, pero no éstas de aquélla. La poesía no es oración, no es rezo; pero el rezo, la oración, cualquier expresión viva de la fe, es siempre poesía; comunicación o comunión recreadora de la creación divina: integración en ella. (pp. 35-36)

It is important to note, then, that Bergamín's intention is always to reveal a process of divinization, the illogical affirmation of the divine in a world which, overtly, is merely human and mortal:

> La fe no se tiene, nos tiene. Y pendientes del tiempo mismo, de nuestra temporalidad. [...] No hay tradición de fe posible para el hombre porque la fe es divina, y aunque al parecer se temporalice en sus creencias, no podrá humanizarse jamás; como no sea en la humanización deshumanizante o deshumanizadora de un Dios 'Hijo del hombre', misterio central del cristianismo, misterio de fe. (p. 26)

Sacrament, as Bergamín describes it in *El clavo ardiendo*, and the resurrection of the body through the crucifixion, is a process of divinization rather than humanization: sacrament is always an opening up to the divine. Sacrament is an essential feature, then, of the dialectics of faith for Bergamín because sacrament requires a going out of oneself, an opening to the divine. It is 'una especie de enfurecimiento, de enajenación racional que se abre al endiosamiento o entusiasmo para poder entrar en su finalidad divina; enterarse o adentrarse, integrarse en su comunicación o comunión con Dios' (p. 31). Thus the transcendent body is divine in nature rather than human. Just as the demonic world is dual in nature, so too is the figure of Christ. The portrayal of religion as anthropology or the humanism inherent in, say, 'personnalisme' or in Tillich's view of religion is what distinguishes these thinkers from Bergamín. He sees the contemplation of the transcendent potential of the body and the bodily nature of poetic, sacred discourse as essential to his dialectics of faith because of the access that the mortification of the flesh provides to transcendence. The resurrection of the flesh and the Word made Flesh are indispensable tropes for Bergamín in his vision of 'at-onement' with God: his is never a purely spiritual quest. Bergamín's quest is always to distil the process by which a dialectical communion is set up and rendered conscious between the temporal and the eternal.

The totality of this communion requires the sacrament of the body and the spirit in favour of an ultimate resurrection of both. It is precisely the incomprehensible nature of such a vision and the seemingly irrational nature of such a quest which differentiates Bergamín's vision, an irrationality which is reflected in Bergamín's approval of an irrational discourse with which to express it:

El lenguaje litúrgico es un lenguaje silencioso porque se dirige a nuestra fe, y no a nuestra razón. [...] Lenguaje de viva poesía, que para encontrar la verdad hay que perder primero la razón: como si la razón fuese su enemigo. [...] Porque la fe no anda los caminos trillados por la razón, sino que se abre en la maleza de lo suyo propio. Como la poesía que la expresa y verifica pareciéndonos que es mentira; como si la verdad tuviera que parecer mentira para serlo de veras. (pp. 47-49)

Bergamín's insistence on the divine orientation of sacrament is a feature of his vision which marks an impassioned reaction to what he sees as the Second Vatican Council's unwarranted deference to the materialism and humanism of the modern world.[6] In *El clavo ardiendo* he eschews any attempt to portray religion as a way of understanding humanity alone and insists upon the fact that any sacrament must be, before all else, an opening up of the Self to the divine. His portrayal of the eucharist, for instance, suggests the possibility of the transformation of the human into the divine rather than the imbibing of the divine into human substance:

En el *gesto* litúrgico, por el contrario, la *señal* de la cruz, el *signo* sacramental, empieza por afirmar en el que lo hace su negación propia: su ensimismamiento y enfurecimiento entusiasta o divino. (p. 43)

The body and the bodily potential of language are therefore given the task of potentiating transcendence through an integration with the divine which in human terms signifies a return to a prelapsarian world where death and reason and, by extension, language (since it mimics mortality in time) are unknown.

The body and the Word made Flesh take part in this dialectical process because they represent the vestiges of the paradise lost and because, in their dual nature, they hold the hidden key to the divine. Again, it is the clash of discourses in language (poetry against rational discourse), and the clash of realities of time (temporality against eternity), which provide the vital spark, the mortification of the body which opens the way to transcendence:

Los extremos se tocan y se entienden. Se identifican. Polarizan, por decirlo así, un idéntico y contradictorio, dramático sentimiento y pensamiento de la vida al expresarla de manera tan extremada. Surge de este contacto el chispazo vivísimo del disparate. Es un cortocircuito imaginativo.[7]

Within the historical context of the Generation of 1927 the notion of poetic discourse as an irrational discourse has as its prime advocate the Surrealist movement. Interestingly the rejection of the hegemony of Reason is accompanied in the Surrealist world by an obsession with images of death and the macabre. Surrealism is often characterized by a fascination with decadence and the mortification of the flesh. Although the movement initially rejected any contemplation of the notion of transcendence, second-wave Surrealism readmits a Hegelian notion of transcendence which is curiously akin to that of Bergamín. It insists upon the placing of the process of transcendence in the material world of things rather than in some outside, other realm.[8]

The materio-mysticism which Robert Havard outlines in the poetry of, for instance, Alberti's *Sobre los ángeles* sites the transformative powers of Alberti's vision within a language which, given free-play, liberates the poet from the tyranny of reason and the constraints of his conscious intellect, forging links between himself and the world that were previously hidden or ridden with decadence (pp. 142-279). Alberti even portrays his discovery symbolically as a type of religious conversion which he attempts to bring to his followers.

Cernuda and Lorca also favour poetic visions which subscribe to a sensual as opposed to an intellectual or conceptual grasp of reality. Metaphor is to them a deeply primitive type of knowledge. By this I mean that for Cernuda and Lorca the poetic image is incarnatory, or iconographic, denoting a containment of essence. For them, the sensual image incarnates reality rather than denoting an emptying of substance such as a symbol might ordinarily suggest. Similarly, Joseph Campbell investigates the mythical nature of metaphor as incarnatory and in reaction to Moyers's comment that a metaphor suggests potential, Campbell replies:

Yes, but it also suggests the actuality that hides behind the visible aspect. The metaphor is the mask of God through which eternity is to be experienced.[9]

Bergamín sees this as the miraculous power of poetry:

La conversión de un *momento histórico* en un *instante eterno* es el milagro naturalmente sobrenatural de la poesía.[10]

And he even portrays poetry itself as a way of acceding to the divine:

Poesía es creación. En dos poetas líricos españoles (los más líricamente puros): Bécquer y San Juan de la Cruz, se afirma este entusiasmo, este entrar en Dios por la poesía, este deificarse o divinizarse por ella. (p. 29)

Despite the proviso that neither Lorca nor Cernuda share Bergamín's religious orientation, there are still similarities of poetic outlook that they appear to have in common. For Cernuda, for instance, all perception is channelled through a perception of sexuality, and for Lorca sensual or carnal perceptions and the pervasive enigma of fate or death, the deeply elemental grooves of human sensibility, form the most reliable though mysterious affirmations of humanity.[11]   Similarly, Bergamín conflates the notions of sexuality and sensuality in the demonic world of his human perceptions, human perceptions which are overshadowed by the persistent spectre of death. Distinctively the world of the senses is the demonic world for him:

Pero como entre sexualidad y sensualidad — dije alguna vez — no hay más que una X de diferencia, que es la incógnita por despejar, nos encontramos con que esta incógnita — la X de la sexualidad — no puede ser despejada más que por el Demonio: porque detrás de esta X, como de toda X, que es una cruz, no puede estar más que el Demonio, no puede haber más que un Demonio.[12]

So Bergamín's poetic instruments are not unusual except for the fact that unlike other poets of the Generation of 1927 the raison d'être of his anti-rational poetic discourse is religious and intensely Christian. Indeed, the sacred nature of this anti-rational poetic discourse underpins and justifies his poetic purpose:

A todos los que pregunten a dónde vamos a parar, o a no parar, con nuestras, más o menos quijotescas, aventuras mundanas; a todos los que nos advierten de nuestra perdición en ellas, debemos contestarles, si son cristianos, con esas palabras goethianas: nos encontraremos en la Cruz.[13]

Unlike Cernuda, Lorca, and even Alberti, Bergamín regards the sensual perceptions of this world as dubious, condemned to being merely a deathly masquerade unless his poetic 'disparates' can succeed in revealing their divine or Christian potential. The poet's sensual world is insufficient for Bergamín. In this sense, Bergamín's poetic vision has as its prerequisite a religious, transcendent purpose. In accordance with his belief, the material world for Bergamín is an illusory world because it is a world of loss, and his poetry, the sacred poetry of sacrament, seeks a realignment of our perceptions and our language with the transcendent realm of the divine, through the Word made Flesh.

Poetic satiation in the Christian sublime signifies a silencing of even the dialectic, of Bergamín's poetic utterance in the greater silence of God:

El universo del cristiano católico, es eso: esa revolucionaria *música celestial* que el incrédulo no percibe: más allá del *silencio eterno de los espacios infinitos* que *le espanta*, no siente esa armonía luminosa de la revolución de los astros, imagen aparente de la *callada música* del Universo, que es una respuesta profunda, silenciosa, de Dios.[14]

Restitution signifies annihilation in human terms, a disturbing predicament but one which for Bergamín is positive as it signifies a resolution of human impotence in the power of the divine. It is, though, with trepidation that Bergamín approaches his salvation because 'la muerte es ruido; la vida es silencio'.[15]

THE FALL INTO REASON

When I speak of Bergamín's urge to return to a world of prelapsarian bliss I assume that the Fall was a fall into death, into the body in time and into reason or knowledge. This knowledge is the knowledge of death, the basis for rational thought being the undeniability of death. The body and language are deathly because they persist in time.

Woman, as symbolically the catalyst of the Fall, is the bringer of death and also of knowledge and utterance. She occupies a symbolic space where she is maligned through her part in the Fall and is forced into becoming a rejection of the feminine, so that the language of the Fall is taken over by a masculine principle of rationality and definition which fears the fluidity and confusion of the feminine.

Paradoxically, then, the feminine is seen as both the cause of knowledge and of utterance in the world and a symbol of a lost fusion of the human with the divine. Turning momentarily to another poet of the Generation of 1927, Carmen Conde, we see in *Mujer sin Edén* the paradoxical situation of woman, especially of Eve, as both the scourge and the salvation of man. As Jo Evans points out in her recent article:

If God and man mirror one another in an 'Extática admiración sin lucha', Man and Eve on the contrary, find in one another a mirroring of the two halves which together make the whole. Thus their mirroring stimulates desire. The narcissistic gaze of the initial relationship, God/man, has only one dynamic, the eternal mirroring of one likeness. In this relationship there can be no communication of meaning. In this way the Fall brings about both the dynamics of desire and of discourse:

> Hermosos caminantes son los ángeles
> que vienen y acompañan nuestro exilio.
> Aquellos de la espada son hostiles,
> severos e implacables; y no duermen.
> Más éstos, no; son instrumentos
> de elocuencia en el brío de sus alas.[16]

Bergamín sees Eve in a similar light, in that she is both the downfall and the salvation of man. The process of separation that began with the birth of Eve from the side of Adam is resolved in the crucifixion, and Bergamín imagistically suggests that as the wound of the Christ parallels Adam's side, so the figure of Eve brings about the escape from mortality, a return to a prelapsarian Eve:

En una sorprendente imagen poética, San Agustín nos simboliza en el agua y la sangre que brotan de la herida del costado del Cristo muerto, el agua bautismal y la sangre eucarística, y, al hacerlo, evoca el origen o nacimiento de la mujer, de Eva, que nace del costado de Adán; o sea, del hombre vivo cuando éste dormía; del costado del hombre dormido (y nos figuramos que soñando — y tal vez soñándola —) nace la mujer como del costado del hombre muerto, o que muere en Cristo, brotan sangre y agua que simbolizan, según el santo, los dos 'sacramentos' de la redención cristiana.[17]

In the same vein, Bergamín's espousal of 'analfabetismo' is a rejection of the deadening structures of intellectual rationality in favour of the intuitive knowledge of innocence:

El poeta añora ignorar, añora la infancia, la inocencia, la ignorancia analfabeta que ha perdido; añora el analfabetismo perdido: la pura razón espiritual de su juego.[18]

Bergamín's 'analfabetismo' offends the abstract rationality of the traditionally male bastions of the pursuit of knowledge and reinvests poetic knowledge as a knowledge which flourishes precisely because of its illogicallity.

Bergamín sees his poetry as the poetry written in old age of the child whose knowledge he has regained with the benefit of hindsight:

Por eso lo que pienso, escribo y siento ahora, a veces les parece a mis lectores un rejuvenecimiento, pero no es tal, es más bien una no vuelta a la niñez, es un encuentro con el lenguaje que en la niñez no se halla y se encuentra a través de una vida muy larga que ha sido toda ella un aprendizaje de escritor.[19]

This poetic knowledge is instinctive and carnal. For Bergamín, reason is pitted against the wisdom of the uncertainty of Faith:

La razón poética de pensar del hombre es su fe. La poesía es siempre de los hombres de fe: nunca de los hombres de letras.[20]

The anti-rational poetics he espouses in his sacred poetry is based upon a Christian notion of resurrection which is sacrificially carnal and sacramentally purifying, an atonement for the Fall, an 'at-onement' with the divine, which ultimately gestures towards a readmittance of the feminine principle of faith as poetic, fluid, infinitely generous, and divine:

Como si con Eva, nacida del costado del hombre dormido, y con la sangre y el agua brotadas por el costado herido del corazón del hombre muerto, se afirmase la humanidad y divinidad de la Iglesia cristiana como presencia temporal simbólicamente femenina, eternamente femenina.[21]

CHRIST AND THE THREE SONNETS

The process of atonement for the Fall is a Christian process for Bergamín. The Word is made Flesh in Christ and the flesh is resurrected in the image of divinity, that of the body which has transcended its mortal, bodily nature. The process of renewal is continual and is represented through the constant contemplation of the crucifixion, death, and resurrection of Christ in the sacrificial and sacramental ritual of the Mass, the incarnation of the Christ in the Eucharist. The figure of Christ is indispensable to any sense of the sacrament: 'Sin el Cristo, fuera del Cristo, carece totalmente de sentido su planteamiento' (*El clavo ardiendo*, p. 67). The central image, as always, is the mortification of Christ's flesh, the fleshly wound which transforms mortality into eternal life:

Santo Tomás nos habla del cáliz y del contenido del cáliz, separándolos previamente para poder unirlos en su significación sacramental, y cita unas palabras de San Juan Crisóstomo apoyando el significado simbólico del cáliz, cuando dice: 'Puesto que es éste el origen de nuestros misterios sagrados (sacramentales), acércate al *temible* cáliz (soy yo quien subraya) como si fuese el costado mismo de Cristo'. (*El clavo ardiendo*, p. 32)

Bergamín sees the crucifixion as the natural resolution of the Fall and, as we have seen, speaks of the Gospel and Genesis in the same breath. Man, if he engages in the quest for eternal life is represented as moving always in a cyclic reflective process, in and out of the reality of mortality and the realm of desire for immortality in the regenerative, creative dialectics of faith.

Rather than static like Christ's Cross, Bergamín's salvationary desire is presented as fluid, moving, and transformative. It is the ritual of sacrifice and sacrament which sets in motion the process of redemption. The urge to incarnation, according to Campbell, requires a fusion of the tree of knowledge and the tree of life, Christ. This can only come about in the material, bodily demonic world, a world of cyclical consumption:

The Christ story involves a sublimation of what originally was a very solid vegetal image. Jesus is on Holy Rood, the tree, and he is himself the fruit of the tree. Jesus is the fruit of eternal life, which was on the second forbidden tree in the Garden of Eden. When man ate of the fruit of the first tree, the tree of the knowledge of good and evil, he was expelled from the Garden. The Garden is the place of unity, of nonduality of male and female, good and evil, God and human beings. You eat the duality, and you are on the way out. The tree of coming back to the Garden is the tree of immortal life, where you know that I and the Father are one.[22]

The emblem of *Cruz y Raya* is that of a tree, and in his *José Bergamín : A Critical Introduction* Nigel Dennis is at pains to explain its significance:

At an early stage in the journal's life, Bergamín decided to use a woodcut of the *hortus philosophae* as a kind of emblem for *Cruz y Raya*. It was another boldly suggestive move on his part. The tree depicted in the woodcut symbolically expressed the scope of the journal's interests and ambitions: the harvesting, as it were, of the fruits of man's labours in areas as far apart as medicine and metaphysics. The logic here, as I have suggested before, was that these disparate disciplines shared a common origin and ultimate purpose, namely the affirmation of human spirituality through creative and critical meditation. The symbol of the tree, however, went much further than that, and Bergamín obviously realized that it had as much exploitable potential as the very title of the journal. The tree also represented nature – the classical source of art — and the process of creation: roots burrowing into the traditions of the past, branches reaching upwards to the sky, which expressed the final goal. The fruits the tree bore and would continue to bear were a sign of cyclical renewal, of man's fertile imagination, and of the promise of his future - a promise reflected in a sense in the first steps taken by the Spanish Republic and the new age it theoretically heralded. In view of these interpretations, it was entirely apt that the publishing offshoot of *Cruz y Raya* should be baptised the Ediciones del Arbol. (p. 156)

I believe that this reading of the tree is only partly true. As I have shown, the orientation of the contributors to *Cruz y Raya* had one essential common principle: 'Para nosotros, la definición *esencial* del espíritu tiene un nombre: Cristo.'[23] Although the *Hortus philosophae* has its roots in knowledge, the basis of the university learning it originally symbolized was Christian. Perhaps, then, the tree was meant to conjure up the image of Christ as well as its more terrestrial reference. In this case, the image of renewal is a Christian image of renewal through sacrifice and resurrection, the countering of disembodied rationality through the material transcendence of the body. The power of the metaphor speaks for itself when we consider the abhorrence with which Bergamín regarded intellectual abstraction, especially as regards the representation of religious ideas:

Nous savons que dans l'Evangile, la prière du Christ demande de nous libérer du Malin et non du Mal: il ne s'agit pas du domaine du Mal, mais du domaine du Malin. [...] Il ne s'agit pas du domaine du Mal, mais du domaine du Malin, ce qui veut dire du domaine du Diable. Cela s'appelle le Monde. [...] Je pense que le Mal est une abstraction. Cette pluralité que Malraux lui donne appartient a une autre réalité qui, pour moi, s'appelle le Malin, le Diable. [...] Parce que le Bien, comme le Mal, est une abstraction. Ces notions tombent dans le domaine juridique, c'est-à-dire moral, du manichéisme. J'oserais dire que Dieu et le Diable sont au-dela du Bien et du Mal.[24]

The culmination of the process towards transcendence is depicted emotively in the three sonnets I introduced in Chapter 1 and they clarify the Christian orientation of Bergamín's vision.[25] I suggested that the poems describe the process of mythical renewal whereby the agonizing Christ is brought to immortality by way of a communion with the feminine principle of the sea. The supremely generous sea transforms the agony of Christ, and the coming into divinity signals a paradoxical acquisition of voice which dissolves distinction, identifying the human and the divine in a oneness which constitutes an atonement, an 'at-onement' which is symbolically portrayed as the merging of the masculine Christ figure with a mythical feminine sea.

We are already prepared for the merciful strength of the sea with the initial epigraph, 'Solo, a lo lejos, el piadoso mar', conjuring up Unamuno and, more distantly, Leopardi.[26] The hesitation and concern of the opening 'No te entiendo, Señor' reminds us that the merging with the divine in individual terms means oblivion and personal annihilation or anonymity, a commonplace trope associated with the sea, 'mortal memoria ante inmortal olvido'. More significantly, Bergamín's 'No te entiendo' is directed at the dead Christ, the mortal Christ, anchored on the cross and like an anchored ship straining against the creative flux of the waters. Stanza two speaks of a familiar feature of Bergamín's vision, his fascination with death, the abandoned Christ of the 'Dios callado', his side hopelessly pierced 'tras el morir, de herida sin respiro'. The poetic persona resides in a state of doubt, or rather incomprehension, in front of the slain Christ and the deathly oblivion of the sea.

Sonnet II changes violently and is addressed to the sea rather than to our Lord. Instead of questioning, the poetic persona exhorts the mother sea to sing a magical, curative song. She is mythical, supernatural, 'madre de monstruos y quimeras', the one who gives birth to radiant music. She is exhorted to sing to the capitalized 'Hombre agonizante' her magical, truthful words. She will be the catalyst of her 'Dios recién nacido', the transforming, paradoxical forces of both death and life. Like the Eve of *El clavo ardiendo*, the sea is both death and resurrection, a fusion of opposites in perpetual creative motion. The Son has escaped her procreative loins:

> Relampaguea, de tormentas suma,
> la faz divinamente atormentada
> del Hijo a tus entrañas evadido.

The sea must whip up a violent storm to match the divine torment, the muted cry for the immortality of the mortal Christ. Her task is to nurture the Godchild into existence, to wash away the curse of death, to rock into oblivion the death of the mortal Christ and produce the new-born God:

> Pulsa la cruz con dedos de tu espuma.
> Y mece por el sueño acariciada,
> la muerte de tu Dios recién nacido.

Turning full circle, the final sonnet is directed to our Lord.   And the poet now beseeches Him to participate in His salvation.   The sea needs the contribution of the Christ figure, the contribution of the humanity of His dying flesh, to complement her spell.   The sea is not a threat nor a challenge to God:

> No se mueven de Dios para anegarte
> las aguas por sus manos esparcidas;
> ni se hace lengua el mar en tus heridas
> lamiéndolas de sal, para callarte.

In fact, she is the feminine divine principle, 'madre de madres', transported by the desire of the Christ to overcome death.   She beseeches the Christ to instigate through his mortal anguish the potential to engender his immortality. Through his bodily anguish he rises again:

> Llega hasta ti la mar, a suplicarte,
> madre de madres por tu afán transidas,
> que ancles en tus entrañas doloridas
> la misteriosa voz con que engendrarte.

But the material flesh must cease to be merely and statically mortal or terrestrial:

> No hagas tu cruz espada en carne muerta;
> mástil en tierra y sequedad hundido;
> árbol en cielo y nubes arraigado.

The Christ will be saved by giving Himself up to the forces of fusion, of fluidity; his mother is the sea, his sacrifice is to her and to an 'at-onement' with her singularity, her totality, the oscillating, ebb and flow of her creative potential, magical, mythical, and enclosing:

> Madre tuya es la mar: sola, desierta.
> Mírala tú que callas, tú caído.
> Y entrégale tu grito arrebatado.

The symbiotic relationship of the feminine and the masculine, of the divine and the human provides the conditions for salvation according to Bergamín's poetic vision of the crucifixion.   This symbiosis, as illustrated in the three sonnets, is always initiated through sacrifice, and is symbolically re-enacted through sacrament.

The centrality of the sacrifice of Christ, the killing, and in the Mass the consumption of the sacrifice, is for Bergamín the pivot of his notion not only of Faith but also of his poetics in that all that is poetic ruptures the carapace of rational materiality, creating a space, a tear in the demonic fabric of human existence and language in which to promote divinity. Religious language, in particular that of the sacrament, is of course necessarily poetic for this reason. The sacrament has to be poetic in order to liberate its divine potential from the demonic masks of language.

The sacrifice of Christ in the crucifixion ruptures the human in order to reveal the divine potential of the Christ, and the consumption of the Eucharist allows the divine to consume the human and atone, and vanquish death. The Word made Flesh integrates the silent word of God with the material jabberings of humanity. As always, the material nature of language is not totally rejected by Bergamín: it constitutes a necessary half of a creative dialectic, the illusory material body which reveals the true, divine potential of its hidden 'soul', as it were.

Bergamín's use of self-consuming imagery and etymological reasoning, his continually vanishing imagery, does the same thing to language as does the reality of the crucifixion and the ritual of the mass. The third poem I cited in this chapter incorporates Calderón's 'siendo un esqueleto vivo,/ siendo un animado muerto' (*Poesías casi completas*, p. 158). This image is generally taken to be a reference to the constant presence of death in life. Bergamín, however, draws it out as an image of eternal life and it is exemplary of the way in which he uses self-consuming imagery in the hope of challenging the mortal predicament of man. The 'esqueleto' image is particularly pertinent in the examination of Bergamín's work because he characterized his persona as skeletal. He elaborates on his self-characterization in an interview with Juan E. González:

— Pero está presente el tema de la muerte...
— Claro. A una de las partes de mi obra la llamo *La vida de un fantasma contada por un esqueleto*, porque yo lo único que tengo, como todo el mundo, es un esqueleto, y ya cada vez menos. [...] Nací esquelético, nunca he tenido carne, nunca he podido creer en la resurrección de la carne. [...] Los esqueletos pensantes ya somos eternos, no le tememos a la muerte ni existe la muerte para los esqueletos pensantes.[27]

Notice that on the one hand Bergamín claims that he cannot believe in the resurrection of the flesh and then, apparently paradoxically, he claims that his skeleton is eternal, thus contradicting the traditional reading of the skeleton as denotative of death. This kind of tortuous double-speak is typical of Bergamín. His real intention is revealed only in his claim that he has never had flesh, only a skeleton. For the reader, then, the two concepts become conflated simply because both images, the flesh and the skeleton, now denote life.

Bergamín's use of an image such as the skeleton, which he makes contain both extremes of life and death, is the tool of his disruptive trade. First, it fits in with his espousal of the illogical as closer to the truth than the rational can be, and second, the at times absurdist and at times remarkably revealing extrapolations in which he indulges, in for instance his literary criticism and poetry, testify to a wish to rupture language and inflict a wound on accepted ways of thinking and expression. This rupturing of semantic security such as we find in the 'esqueleto' image throws Bergamín into the realm of the fantastic. It is an attempted mysticism based on the belief that language can be made to express what is outside the realm of human understanding: the divine. Bergamín's exhilarating and infuriating wordplay is an attempt to make language mean more, especially when using metaphorical terms. It is as though he is subjecting poetic language to a type of transubstantiation. Françoise Meltzer sees the self-consuming pun as having a parallel purpose: 'Within this system, that "gap" in metaphor, that *in absentia*, is repressed and becomes *in praesentia*.'[28] And indeed, it would seem that what Bergamín seeks with his disruptive 'disparates' is, rather than disintegration of original referential potency, a type of supplementarity which adds to rather than detracts from signification. Again, such a reading not only accords with my reading of the imagery of the 'Tres sonetos' but also with Meltzer's assessment of the underlying imperative of Lacan's self-consuming puns. For Meltzer too, as for Bergamín, such linguistic devices attempt to 'allow for moments of "grace"':

By 'mysticism', I mean Lacan's attempt to 'rupture' the (male) economy of totality by means of a fantasy of supplementarity — precisely as he argues, in 'The Woman', when describing the woman's *jouissance*. I will propose that we see the pun in Lacan as an attempt to overcome analogy (totality) with supplementarity — an economy of contiguity which will, ultimately, allow for moments of 'grace'. (p. 157)

Bergamín is involved in a paradoxical quest for incarnation through the rupturing of the masculinity of rationality. Poetic language must be sacred, purifying, and purified of rationality, the curse of the Fall. It must bring about presence rather than absence, signification must not be continually escaping into death. In his poetry the process of restitution is articulated as a continual rebirth, as we see in the Spring poems of *Duendecitos y Coplas*. In *El aposento en el aire: Introducción a la poesía de José Bergamín* Nigel Dennis examines the renewal or rebirth that overcomes death:

Empieza el poema describiendo la presencia de una primavera oculta dentro de la escena invernal que contempla:
> Esta tarde de Invierno una invisible
> Primavera aletea con los pájaros...
El poeta presiente la revivificación que se esconde detrás o dentro de la desnudez aparentemente estéril de la escena. La inminencia del renacimiento le consuela y alienta, dándole una especie de garantía de que la muerte puede superarse:

Un renacer de nueva Primavera
el Invierno parece estar soñando
como si de otro sueño más profundo
se hubiese despertado.
Fuerte, más fuerte que la muerte, el alma
la deja que se acerque paso a paso.

La frase clave es, por supuesto, '*más fuerte que la muerte*': la afirmación categórica ('...ya sé ahora, por fin...') del triunfo de la vida sobre la muerte. (pp. 102-03)

Rather like the skeleton image, the image of winter according to Bergamín holds in latency its own antidote, the spring. This is, then, a poetry of a paradoxical form of affirmation which denies reason and functions as an affirmation of faith in the face of the apparent degeneration of material reality. Bergamín's religious reading of the human condition and his conceptual representation of the functioning of language in poetic discourse is united in the continual physical rebirth of spring as a sacred process, the birth of possibility from death, the positive supplementary promise contained in winter.

The figuring of the resurrection of the Christ is a central figure in Bergamín's dialectics of Faith. In addition, his poetic discourse, as a supreme discourse, is the linguistic counterpart of this figuring. The notion of fluidity inherent in the dialectic and the slippery nature of language is essential to this vision: the 'desengaño' is constant and the maintenance of this oscillating vision is the key to Bergamín's desired access to the divine.

The static nature of the traditional representation of the religious figures must be undermined in order to promote this fluid image. The repetitive and rewritten contemplation of death, the attempted sublimation of death in his poetry, the destabilizing of the supposedly rigid materiality of human reality and symbolization, are brought under continual attack through the mockery of rationality, which is ever present in Bergamín's poetic utterance. The reader is compelled to realign, to rupture the beating of the 'dance macabre', and to force into being a sublime vision which is ultimately a vision of supplementarity, provided through rupture, through the mortification of the flesh. It is a vision which is imagistically portrayed in the three sonnets at least as a readmittance of the feminine which is a realm of generosity, 'the realm of the gift', of the divine.[29]

NOTES

[1] José Bergamín, *El clavo ardiendo,* with a preface by André Malraux (Barcelona: Aymá, 1974), pp. 111-12.

[2] José Bergamín, 'La razón de soñar', in *Beltenebros y otros ensayos sobre literatura española* (Barcelona and Madrid: Noguer, 1973), pp. 89-93 (p.89). Henceforth *Beltenebros.*

[3] In *El clavo ardiendo* Bergamín observes: 'En el misterioso lenguaje litúrgico sacramental, el que lo

inteligible se nos haga sensible por la poesía nos parece mentira. Una mentira que nos trasparenta la verdad enmascarándola paradójicamente para desenmascararse mejor, como en el teatro' (p. 50).

4 *El clavo ardiendo*, p. 39.

5 Octavio Paz, *Conjunctions and Disjunctions*, trans. by Helen Lane (New York: Arcade Publishing, 1990), p. 14.

6 *El clavo ardiendo* constitutes an attack upon the Second Vatican Council's laicization of the sacraments. Bergamín sees the demystification of religious practices, exemplified for instance by the introduction of Eucharistic ministers, as fundamentally opposed to the essence of the Christian sacraments, the aim of which he considers to be divinization of the human rather than anthropomorphism of the divine.

7 José Bergamín, 'El disparate en la literatura española', in *Al fin y al cabo (Prosas)* (Madrid: Alianza, 1981), pp. 29-57 (p. 35).

8 See Chapter 7 in Robert G. Havard, *From Romanticism to Surrealism: Seven Spanish Poets* (Cardiff: University of Wales Press, 1988), pp.242-79, for an analysis of Breton's manifestos, the first influenced largely by Freud and the second under the ascendancy of Hegel, and in which, according to Havard, 'the Surrealist image — which treats the object as an object, never an abstraction — [is] a confirmation of Hegel's metaphysic of the phenomenology of mind, that is, of materio-mysticism, which Breton described in the second manifesto as 'the penetrability of subjective life by 'substantial' life''' (p. 247).

9 Joseph Campbell, with Bill Moyers, *The Power of Myth*, p. 60.

10 José Bergamín, 'De la naturaleza y figuración fronteriza de la poesía', in *Beltenebros y otros ensayos sobre literatura española*, pp. 9-75 (p. 18).

11 See Angel Sahuquillo, *Federico García Lorca y la cultura de la homosexualidad: Lorca, Dalí, Cernuda, Gil-Albert, Prados y la voz silenciada del amor homosexual* (Stockholm: Stockholms Universitet, 1986). Sahuquillo cites the following words of Lorca: 'En mi lira tengo yo el secreto de las pasiones - dice David - [...] Vuestro gran pecado ha sido desligar la carne del espíritu. [...] Porque, en verdad os digo que vosotros sois los que necesitáis de la misericordia de la carne'; and of Cernuda: 'En otra ocasión lo has dicho: nada puedes percibir, querer, ni entender si no entra en ti primero por el sexo, de ahí al corazón y luego a la mente. Por eso tu experiencia, tu acorde místico, comienza como una prefiguración sexual' (p. 7).

12 José Bergamín, 'La importancia del demonio', in *La importancia del demonio y otras cosas sin importancia* (Madrid: Júcar, 1974), p. 116.

13 José Bergamín, *Aforismos de la cabeza parlante* (Madrid: Turner, 1983), pp. 22-23.

14 José Bergamín, 'La callada de Dios' (August 1935), reprinted in *'Cruz y Raya': Antología*, pp. 419-25 (pp. 419-20).

15 *El clavo ardiendo*, p. 45.

16 Jo Evans, 'Carmen Conde's *Mujer sin Edén*: Controversial Notions of "Sin"', in *Women Writers in Twentieth-century Spain and Spanish America*, ed. by Catherine Davies (Lewiston, MD: Mellen, 1993), pp. 71-83 (p. 78).

17 *El clavo ardiendo*, p. 33.

18 José Bergamín, 'La decadencia del analfabetismo', in *La importancia del demonio y otras cosas sin importancia*, pp. 31-53 (p. 38).

19 Juan E. González, 'Entrevista con José Bergamín', *Nueva Estafeta*, no. 4 (March 1979), 51-55 (p. 55).

20 José Bergamín, 'La decadencia del analfabetismo', p. 50.

21 *El clavo ardiendo*, p. 33.

22 Joseph Campbell, with Bill Moyers, *The Power of Myth*, p. 107.

23 *Cruz y Raya*, 15 April 1933, p. 10.

24 *Malraux, celui qui vient: Entretiens entre André Malraux, Guy Saurès, José Bergamín*, ed. by Guy Saurès (Paris: Stock, 1979), p. 57.

25 See Juan Guillermo Renart, 'Los "Tres sonetos a Cristo crucificado ante el mar", comienzo público del Bergamín poeta', in *Camp de l'arpa*, nos. 67-68 (September 1979), 27-33. In this article Renart takes a contrary view to my own, namely that the sea is monovalent, signifying only death.

26 'Tres sonetos a Cristo crucificado ante el mar', *Poesías casi completas*, pp. 23-24.

27 Juan E. González, 'Entrevista con José Bergamín', pp. 54-55.

28 Françoise Meltzer, 'Eat Your *Dasein*: Lacan's Self-Consuming Puns', in *On Puns: The Foundation of Letters*, ed. by Jonathan Culler (Oxford: Blackwell, 1988), pp. 156-63 (p. 159).

29 See Toril Moi's explanation of Hélène Cixous's distinction between the 'Realm of the Proper' and the 'Realm of the Gift' in Toril Moi, *Sexual/Textual Politics: Feminist Literary Theory*, pp. 110-13.

CHAPTER 5

BERGAMIN AND THE EXILIC IMAGINATION

And we are no more doomed really than anyone, as we go
together, through this moon terrain
where everything is dry and perishing and so
vivid, into the dunes, vanishing out of sight,
vanishing out of the sight of each other,
vanishing even out of our own sight,
looking for water.
        Margaret Atwood [1]

THE EXILIC WORLD OF POETRY

In order to reassess Christian symbology, in the way I outlined in the previous
chapter, and rescue its potential through art, through poetry, Bergamín has to
reassess language in terms of human estrangement.[2]   He has to revise the
notion of objectivization; he has to reject individuality in favour of
individuation, fusion, con-fusion. This is an acceptance of abjection and exile
as the prerequisites for his utopian quest, his flight towards the sublime, a
merging of the soul with the great soul, God, in opposition to an
objectivization of the material world. This constitutes a re-engagement of the
feminine. Such a figuring of Bergamín's poetic works is a defence of and
justification for his glossing of other poets as part of his rejection of traditional
notions of identity and definition in favour of fusion and unicity of voice
projected towards the divine.

   If one is to examine Bergamín's poetry in terms of human estrangement, one
is inevitably struck by the notion of place and its relationship to human
identity. Bergamín, we shall see, conflates the two preoccupations into the
image of dream, of 'sueño'; his place of being and identity is often seen as the
place or non-place of dream. To speak of place at the same time as speaking
of exile or estrangement is to circle a paradox, to talk about places that are not
places or rather are the places of displacement commonly referred to in exilic
writing.

   Hélène Cixous posits the twentieth century as the century of exile and the
century of exilic writing. For Cixous the writer is, essentially, an exile whose
place of exile is writing itself.[3] Writing designates a place of exile as well as a
place for the exile, a paradoxical haven or asylum, an alternative place of

belonging. For Bergamín, exile is the preternatural state of Man, who is exiled from the divine. Metaphorically speaking, we shall see that such radical unbelonging is akin to an expulsion *into* human life and a banishment from the maternal womb. Exile is the natural state of the poet whose task it is to create a place of assurance in his writing. Along with political exile, these different states of exile shape Bergamín's attitude to the notion of 'place' in his poetry.

The place from which one is exiled is important simply because exile is usually looked upon in terms of loss, in terms of what or where one is exiled from, so confusion in this area is bound to cloud our view of the poetry itself. However, one of my main points is that criticism all too often focuses on the source of exile when in fact the poet is focusing on the destiny of exile, the place that has been arrived at through exile. The writer constructs both a poetic identity and a poetry as separate and autonomous from himself or herself. This conscious distancing is necessary if writing is to constitute a salvation or a freeing of the poet from an exilic state, or simply and more realistically, a poetic accommodation to the state of exile. Bergamín's and, similarly, Paul Celan's poetic testimonies express themselves as a reversal, revolution, and redefinition of exile as a positive or fomentive state, a change of attitude, a strange sort of solace brought about through the writing-out of exile.

Both Bergamín and Celan consciously extend a poetic persona to the public: Celan, 'ce land', creates a name for himself as 'this land', a land which is a person, but a land which is called Lost and which is No-one.[4] Bergamín continually refers to himself in poetic terms, creating a personal symbology out of his 'peregrino' status, as a 'fantasma', an 'esqueleto vivo', an 'ensimismado' living the deferred life of a pilgrim; in some senses, where he is heading for is more important than where he has come from. Most significantly, though, for Bergamín, Man himself is as much a place as a person, for he resides in the place of dreaming, an insubstantial place denoting the insubstantiality of life, an insubstantiality which can only be resolved by death:

El hombre que vive, sueña. El hombre vive lo que sueña. El hombre empieza por vivir lo que sueña, y acaba por soñar lo que vive. Empieza por soñar lo que es y acaba por ser lo que sueña. Empieza y acaba por ser sueño o por soñarlo ser. [...] ¿Qué puerta encontraremos para salir de este conceptuoso laberinto en que nos adentra el poeta con su conocida comedia, con todas sus comedias, de sueño, de vida? Puerta secreta, escondida, tapada. Puerta de perdido paraíso. Puerta que una sola vez pasaremos. Una vez para nunca más. Puerta de la muerte.[5]

Returning to the notion of a necessary distance between the poet and poetry, it would be erroneous to assume that the degree of poetic intensity on the part of the poet, as exhibited in the work of either Celan or Bergamín, means that the poet himself cannot distinguish between Self and writing. I am inclined to think that both Bergamín's and Celan's projections of Self as less than whole people, as exiles, as the poetic personae of loss, are an attempt to state and move on, to step past their archetype and force their readers to focus not on the circumstantial, factual reality of their personal exiles, but rather on the nature and potency of their place of writing, of their consolation or reception of loss. As with any label, the label of exile can blind the reader to reality.

Poetry tries to place reality as if it were not already placed, indeed, assuming that it is not placed. John Berger salutes the necessary presence of poetry, stating that:

Poems, regardless of any outcome, cross the battlefields, tending the wounded, listening to the wild monologues of the triumphant or the fearful. They bring a kind of peace. Not by anaesthesia or easy reassurance, but by recognition and the promise that what has been experienced cannot disappear as if it had never been. [...] The promise is that language has acknowledged, has given shelter, to the experience which demanded, which cried out.[6]

Poetry for Berger houses that which is under threat of oblivion, thus making it the place of banishment. Perhaps this notion could also include Catherine Clément's observation that 'somewhere every culture has an imaginary zone for what it excludes'.[7]

The persistence with which Bergamín is condemned by his critics to the status of a 'poeta exiliado' means that his personal identity and his personality are continually brought to bear on his writing. It could be said that the resultant confusion of the different states of political exile and ontological exile brings about in the reader's mind a confusion of the notions of eternity or eternal life with literary immortality, which potentially undermines Bergamín's status as a poet. This would not matter if for Bergamín poetry and the place of writing were not dependent upon his distancing of language from Self. In fact, Bergamín seeks a new Self in the exile of writing. This new Self is different from his personal, alienated, temporally-bound self. Both Bergamín and Celan privilege language over their privileged status as poets in their quest to find this new eternal Self . The problem, however, is perennial. Mercedes Cárdenas, in an article on Cernuda, also an exile in all senses, draws the distinction between the poet's preoccupation with immortality and with eternity: 'La eternidad, no la inmortalidad, es para Cernuda la búsqueda de la trascendencia en la idea de un tiempo abstracto e inalterable.'[8] For Berger, too, it is language rather than the poet that testifies to exile:

The poet places language beyond the reach of time: or, more accurately, the poet approaches language as if it were a place, an assembly point, where time has no finality, where time itself is encompassed and contained. [...] Poetry can speak of immortality because it abandons itself to language, in the belief that language embraces all experience, past, present, and future. [...] It is precisely the co-existence of future, present, and past that poetry proposes. A promise that applies to the present and past as well as to the future can better be called an assurance. (pp. 22-23)

Obviously, both Bergamín and Celan contextualize their poetry historically. Celan is intensely aware of writing post-holocaust but only George Steiner and perhaps Michael Hamburger think that now it is impossible to be convinced by the illusion of civilization post-holocaust.[9] But human nature does not change; we are amnesiac by nature. Celan, however, Celan in name and nature, dates himself differently; he may be an original exile, a son of the diaspora as well as the holocaust, but he is also simply a modern man and God-forsaken, as he seems to be saying in 'OVER WINE AND LOSTNESS, over the running-out of both':

> I rode through the snow, do you hear,
> I rode God into farness ⸱ nearness, he sang,
> it was
> our last ride over
> the human hurdles.
>
> They ducked when
> they heard us above their heads, they
> wrote, they
> lied our whinnying
> into one
> of their be-imaged languages.[10]

He is God-forsaken, and Modernity will not allow adequate expression of that.

Similarly, Bergamín, also an exile, eager to belong to the company of Republican outcasts, predates his exile. He is an eternal pilgrim, an eternal exile, because he is God-forsaken. His pilgrim status informs his attitude to his existential estrangement from his homeland, Spain:

> Fui peregrino en mi patria
> desde que nací:
> Y fui en todos los tiempos
> que en ella viví.
>
> Lo sigo siendo al estarme,
> ahora y aquí,
> peregrino de una España
> que ya no está en mí.
>
> (*Poesía, VII*, p. 30)

Here Bergamín's 'ya no está' begs the question, was Spain ever in him? In his political as well as his poetic writing Bergamín appears to be trying to fill the void where his nationality should be. He feels an instinctive need, an imperative to express his Spanishness, his statement and need serving only to crystallize a sense of lack, of loss. And Spanishness for Bergamín is of course associated with Christianity, the lack of Spain being inextricably linked with estrangement from God. Spanish poetry for Bergamín is quintessentially Christian:

¿No arraiga el pensamiento mismo en su disparatado empeño humano de hacerse divino o ansia divina de ser humano? ¿No es éste el disparate humano y divino — religioso y cristiano — más disparatado de todos, el disparate de los disparates? El disparate total y único: totalizador y unificador; el disparate verdadero, el disparate *como un templo*. Pues en este humano radicalismo disparatado de lo humano, que es el cristianismo, se encierra, a mi parecer, el secreto, el secreto a voces — el equívoco espiritual y verbal de toda nuestra poesía española: la más humana por más cristiana, la más española, también, por eso. Es ésta la razón de ser de todas las formas disparatadas de esta poesía, de todos estos disparatados lenguajes poéticos.[11]

According to Sïan Miles, Simone Weil makes a similar connection in *The Need for Roots*:

In *The Need for Roots*, she defines the crime of uprooting which, whether it be in seventeenth century Italy or twentieth century South Africa, consists in the destruction of physical links with the past and dissolution of the community. She claims that loss of the past in this way is the equivalent of loss of the supernatural, i.e. that through which it is demonstrable that the good is different from necessity and whereby the dead can speak with an authentic voice to the living.[12]

PRETERNATURAL EXILE

It may be psychoanalytically accurate to diagnose the exilic imagination as a preternatural exile; the state of mind produced by the expulsion from the maternal womb. However, here we speak of an interpretation which seems to be contradicted by the fact that original exile is so forcefully described by Bergamín as an exile from God. It is only when one sees that the exile from God is expressed precisely as preternatural exile, given that the divine is imaged as feminine, that it becomes possible to see these two forms of exile as essentially synonymous, as Bergamín describes in the three sonnets I examined in the last chapter.

Male poets actually voice exile as an exile from God, rather than as an exile from the womb. And even if God were a woman or 'J' was a woman who invented God, male poetic preoccupations seem to be not so much to do with birth as with death.[13] Christiane Rochefort would have us believe that this distinction between birth and death signals the fact that there is a gendered difference in experience as well as in language:

Has literature a sex? With dignity, I, and most of my sisters, we would answer: No. But. But. But, do we have the same experience? Do we have the same mental structures? The same obsessions? Death, for instance, is a specifically male obsession. As well as essential solitude. After all, we don't belong to the same civilisation.[14]

However, such a reading is purely materialist, has very little to do with the spiritual preoccupations of Bergamín, and denies the cyclical, fluid vision of his religious perspective: birth implies death, a beginning calling an end, and beginnings and endings imply inevitably a sense of loss. The image of loss conflates the exile from God with the exile from the mother's womb, both of which can only be remedied through death. Both condemn one to an individuality which denies fusion with the Other.

Bergamín's place in the poetic tradition, along with his religious preoccupation with death, further substantiates his apparent delectation for the death motif. The naming of his book *Esperando la mano de nieve* is taken from Bécquer and the Romantic tradition, which of course sees death as a prime mover of poetic inspiration, as Salinas explains in his analysis of Jorge Manrique:

A great Spanish poet of the nineteenth century, Bécquer, compared genius with a harp, asleep in a dark corner of a salon, its chords full of marvelous notes awaiting 'a hand of snow that may awake them.' Jorge Manrique's case is a perfect illustration of Bécquer's harp. He spent most of his life asleep, in a courtly salon. And two years before his death he found the mysterious hand, the real hand of snow since it was the hand of death, that awakened all the slumbering music so that we shall never forget it.[15]

Life for Bergamín and Celan is in effect a land called Lost, and language is a place, *the* place of being (for Celan language was the only thing that remained intact for him after the war).[16] *The* place of being, the only asylum in the land called Lost which restitutes up to a point, which consoles, assures, and mourns loss. For Bergamín, language at least provides hope:

> Tus palabras, poeta,
> no son más que palabras:
> pero tiene el oído
> que aprender a escucharlas,
>
> para oír esa música
> tan sonora y tan clara
> como la voz del viento,
> como la voz del agua;

son palabras tan hondas
que le llegan al alma
tal vez para decirle
lo que el corazón calla.

(*Poesía, II*, p. 65)

Life is no longer positive and vital.   On the one hand it is a place of
banishment, expulsion and on the other it is a prison from which access to
eternity is only afforded by the breaching of the unknowable wall of death.
Faced with such annihilation, the exilic imagination searches for a sublime
place of restitution, and this place is for Bergamín the place of language, the
apparently impossible place of poetry.

ABJECTION AND LANGUAGE

In his poetry Bergamín presents us with a world in which the literary persona
is in some way divorced from reality, or the place it wants to be.   It cannot
communicate with that world or its inhabitants: or rather its inhabitants are like
the literary persona itself, lost voices with only a shadowy perception of the
world and each other.   This raises the more than academic question of why
Bergamín writes.   For whom is he writing if the other inhabitants of his world
can understand but feebly?

The poet answers this problem by creating a positive world out of his
poetry, a place from his displacement. That is to say, in his poetry he creates a
separate place or process from which he views the essentially negative fact of
his exile.   I hope to demonstrate the essential paradox of this effort. For by
creating and eternalizing this place Bergamín traps himself in the exile,
displacement, or non-place, of which the poetic place is a reflection, is a mirror
image.

Bergamín's poetry narrates a history of contradiction, the contradiction of
exile and imprisonment, movement, wandering, and constraint.   His poetry
enacts a Kafkaesque angst in a battle with outmoded ontological weapons
against imprisonment at the hands of language, which is obsolete for all but the
task of imprisonment.   If Bergamín can claim to achieve any personal victory
through his angst, it is a victory won largely by default where, too exhausted to
fight against the linguistic fragmentation and ontological disintegration of his
identity, even as his struggle against it contributes to it, the poet recoups a
sense of cohesion from the very agent of his imprisonment. That agent is the
obsolescence of a language alienated from, rather than correlative with, any
true sense of Being or Reality:

El hombre desde que nace
le va huyendo a su destino:
y por quererle escapar
le va abriendo más caminos.[17]

In addition:

Voy huyendo de mi voz,
huyendo de mi silencio;
huyendo de las palabras
vacías con que tropiezo.

Como si no fuera yo
el que me voy persiguiendo,
me encuentro huyendo de mí
cuando conmigo me encuentro.

(*Poesía, II*, p. 28)

Bergamín's stance is similar to Kristeva's notion of abjection, a questioning stance which asks not who but where?:

The one by whom the abject exists is thus a *deject* who places (himself), *separates* (himself), situates (himself), and therefore *strays* instead of getting his bearings, desiring, belonging, or refusing. Situationist in a sense, and not without laughter — since laughing is a way of placing or displacing abjection. Necessarily dichotomous, somewhat Manichaean, he divides, excludes, and without, properly speaking, wishing to know his abjections is not at all unaware of them. Often, moreover, he includes himself among them, thus casting within himself the scalpel that carries out his separations. Instead of sounding himself as to his 'being', he does so concerning his place: *'Where* am I?' instead of *'Who* am I?' For the space that engrosses the deject, the excluded, is never *one*, nor *homogeneous*, nor *totalizable*, but essentially divisible, foldable and catastrophic. A diviser of territories, languages, works, the *deject* never stops demarcating his universe whose fluid confines — for they are constituted of a non-object, the abject — constantly question his solidity and impel him to start afresh. A tireless builder, the deject is in short a *stray*. He is on a journey, during the night, the end of which keeps receding. He has a sense of the danger, of the loss that the pseudo-object attracting him represents for him, but he cannot help taking the risk at the very moment he sets himself apart. And the more he strays, the more he is saved.[18]

The concept of Self as selflessness, as Kristeva describes it, makes a positive of a negative when it is applied, for instance, to mystical figures. We shall see that what appears to be an entirely negative figuring of selfhood for Bergamín in his poetry is actually his valiant attempt to overcome his exile from God. This is a rejection of selfhood in favour of fusion, a going out of himself towards the divine. In addition, Kristeva suggests that the abject personality, founded as it is on the notion of loss, conceives the only valid form of expression as one which sets up a dialectical creative process of meaning based on that assumption of loss and the need for restitution. Loss then becomes the propellor of utterance, and in poetic terms this is true also of Bergamín's poetic production:

If it be true that the abject simultaneously beseeches and pulverises the subject, one can understand that it is experienced at the peak of its strength when that subject, weary of fruitless attempts to identify with something on the outside, finds the impossible within; when it finds that the impossible constitutes its very *being*, that it *is* none other than abject. The abjection of self would be the culminating form of that experience of the subject to which it is revealed that all its objects are based merely on the inaugural *loss* that laid the foundations of its own being. There is nothing like the abjection of self to show that all abjection is in fact recognition of the *want* on which any being, meaning, language, or desire is founded. (p. 5)

THE PILGRIMAGE OF THE SUBLIME

A poetry of flight, the poems themselves become, paradoxically, the weightless stones of the wall that Bergamín constructs in self-defence against a hostile world. In other words, the poems become a truer place than the non-place, the shifting sands, which the poems describe:

> Pasa la vida pero no volando
> porque al pasar y no pasar sin vuelo
> su paso va posándose en el suelo
> y a su pesar en él se va quedando.
> Pasa y al corazón le va pesando
> como a los ojos pesa el mar o el cielo:
> como le pesa al alma su desvelo
> de un pesaroso sueño despertando.
>
> A su paso, a su peso van cayendo
> las horas muertas de un vivir que ha sido
> por un fue y un será lo que está siendo
>
> como una suave música al oído,
> un día y otro día desviviendo
> 'de la risa del alba al sol dormido'.

(Poesía, I, p. 48)

The dual meaning of 'flight' in English is an ironic pointer to a semantic conceit in Bergamín's thought. Flight ('vuelo') is conceived as a definition of the sublime in Art, and he says:

Poetry has been defined as a 'form of flight' — which is the exact opposite of a flight from form. He who flees form escapes life and dies. He who gives his flight — his personal flight — form will survive in this form, even if he dies.[19]

The form of flight ('vuelo') sets the artist above man, and flight ('huida') from the 'form of flight' (the creation of personal art) condemns man to his mortality. As in the previous poem, the lack of flight ('vuelo') weighs Man down to a terrestrial existence and yet the achievement of flight ('vuelo') is often only construed as 'huida', a negative flight from destiny, that is from death. However, this 'huida' opens, as 'vuelo', salvationary possibilities:

> Y por quererle escapar
> le va abriendo más caminos.
>
> (*Duendecitos y coplas*, p. 34)

And:

> Nadie encuentra su camino.
> El camino se hace huyendo
> del camino. Y el pensar
> huyendo del pensamiento.
>
> (*Duendecitos y coplas*, p. 18)

Flight ('huida') therefore has both negative and positive connotations, fleeing away and flying towards, fleeing the terrestrial and confronting the sublime. The reason for the apparent confusion is rooted, therefore, in the fact that both expressions refer to the same action. It is merely a matter of perspective.

Bergamín's fascination with the concept of flight reflects his preoccupation with imperatives. It is one of the axes of his thought, a rumination around the moment and wherefore of life's decisions. Like Picasso, his realm of thought is both artistic and political, and each sphere is dependent upon attitudes to the notion of free movement. Art and Liberty are concepts in common according to Picasso, who claims:

The point is, art is something subversive. It's something that should *not* be free. Art and Liberty, like the fire of Prometheus, are things one must steal, to be used against the established order.[20]

Struggle supplies life with its energy. Bergamín's raison d'être perishes in the face of cohesion, freedom, and tranquillity. This means there is a fear of resolution implicit in his stance towards all aspects of creative and political life. This fear creates a blindness that undercuts his most perceptive statements and this blindness constitutes the nearest the twentieth century can get to tragedy. This tragedy consists in the fact that by forming a consolation for, or a means of coping with his exile, man becomes entrapped in that exile. By becoming a poet in order to cope with his sense of exile, Bergamín is forced to live with his exile, to come to terms with it but not to resolve it.

Bergamín's poetry is oppositional in the sense that its task is to obstruct contact and to create it simultaneously. The poet's quest is to make semantic obstruction palpable in his poetry in order, ultimately, to confirm a new contact which is more effective and honest, perhaps, than the blurred distinctions between Being and Non-being which are   ordinarily afforded to the poet by the 'contact' between the 'I' and the world:

> De corazón a corazón,
> de pensamiento a pensamiento,
> mi palabra va a tu palabra
> y mi silencio a tu silencio.
>
> Como si tu voz en mi voz
> fuese sólo un eco en el eco;
> como si callando los dos
> hablásemos al mismo tiempo.   (*Poesía, I,* p. 260)

Also:

> A fuerza de decirlas tantas veces
> no queda en las palabras
> más que el hueco sonoro de un silencio
> poblado de fantasmas.
>
> Un espectral reflejo, fugitivo
> como sombra de nube por el agua.
> Y sin la voz ni el rostro que lo llene
> el vacío de la máscara.
>
> (*Poesía, I,* p. 256)

The inefficacy of communication is one of the main themes of Bergamín's poetry and the 'fantasma' is his predominant leitmotif. These aspects of his work are complex, however, not least because the `fantasma' persona is for Bergamín a positive image of the role of the artist and of art. He states in his essay 'Transparent Masks: Reflections on Picasso's Personality':

At a seance, Victor Hugo heard the voice of a mysterious personage claiming to be Death, who announced that every spirit performs two tasks in his existence, one as a human, the other as a ghost. This is true of every artist, writer, or thinker, who in his creative role performs the ghostly task.   Hence every intellectual creation of man seems to us illusionistic. The visages of painting and poetry, prose and music, are all transparent masks. (p. 13)

The weightless stones of Bergamín's wall of self-defence, his poems, are what detain him on the site of battle, in the process of defence, thwarting his flight ('huida'), constituting his poetic flight ('vuelo'), and eventually imprisoning him in the moment of indecision, in the clarity of the contradictory forces and perspectives of flight. Neither flight is fully achieved, though each is forever necessary, imminent, feared, barely there on the site of the battle. It is the barely-thereness of Bergamín's poetry which is intimately linked with the concept of exile in his poetry. The Spain Bergamín yearns for is barely there:

> Una peregrina tan peregrina,
> que iba sola.
>
> Cervantes

> Peregrina su voz como una sombra
> por las tan peregrinas soledades
> de las tierras de España, como el vuelo
> perdido de las aves
> o el paso del rebaño luminoso
> de las nubes errantes.
> Espaciosas y tristes lejanías
> iluminan y abren
> al sueño quijotesco de su alma
> el alma del paisaje.
> Vida, luz y verdad fueron camino
> de sus peregrinantes:
> Sigismundas, Persiles....hiperbóreos
> testigos fantasmales
> de una España tan sola y peregrina
> como su voz distante.
>
> (*Poesía, I*, p. 209)

'El alma del paisaje', the notions of place and placelessness are central to Bergamín's poetry. For him, Being itself is a place lost, mourned, and, through mourning, potentially restituted. Bergamín's poetry embodies a confrontational stance which both condemns and liberates him to the exilic, to the place of dissidence which is at once no place at all and yet the only place where he can salvage his vestigial personal identity. Exile locates a haven for any potential assimilation of the symbolic disintegration that haunts him:

> Este 'ahora' y 'aquí' que nunca han sido
> y que nunca serán, que no están siendo,
> abren al 'yo', fantasma que los sueña,
> un hueco sepulcral para su sueño.
>
> (*Poesía, I*, p. 89)

And:

> Una voz que no encuentra
> aposento en el aire
> es una voz perdida
> que no oye nunca nadie.
> Su sonido se apaga
> en los ecos distantes.
> Y las sombras se llevan
> sus palabras errantes.

(Poesía, I, p. 91)

In reaction to such linguistic flimsiness, the condition of exile instigates in Bergamín his only vocal, and quasi-physical strength as he haunts society as the phantom that disturbs the false consciousness of the home from which he himself is eternally debarred. Exiled, Bergamín always functions 'as if dead':

> Yo soy un muerto, y a un muerto
> no debe importarle nada
> de la vida, ni siquiera
> llevar su muerte en el alma.
>
> Que estar muerto es estar solo
> y la soledad se basta
> y se sobra para ser
> una muerte que no acaba.

(Poesía, IV, p. 99)

Or:

> Me estoy mirando al espejo
> y en mi rostro envejecido
> veo la cara de un muerto.
>
> Y miro todo mi cuerpo
> como un fantasma irrisorio
> de huesos y de pellejo.[21]

The potential restitution of lost identity through a re-placing of the Self is poignantly expressed in Paul Celan's poem 'Eis, Eden'. Celan voices the preoccupations of Bergamín with his definitive metaphor of 'a land called Lost'. 'Eis, Eden' may act as an imagistic point of comparison for the consideration of the exilic in Bergamín's imagination:

> There is a country Lost,
> a moon grows in its reeds,
> where all that died of frost
> as we did, glows and sees.

It sees, for it has eyes,
each eye an earth, and bright.
The night, the night, the lyes.
This eye-child's gift is sight.

It sees, it sees, we see,
I see you, you see me.
Before this hour has ended
ice will rise from the dead.[22]

SOLITUDE AS THE ABSENCE OF GOD

The movement towards restitution of identity in Celan's poem is inconceivable
without the original loss of place, loss of Self, just as the movement of man's
utterance to sublime expression in art is meaningless without a preconditional
banality of humanity, just as salvation and life eternal is inconceivable without
the Fall and Christ's promise of immortality. The movement from loss to gain,
from meaninglessness to meaningfulness is Bergamín's main focus. With
reason Bergamín identifies himself strongly with Picasso in his essay
'Transparent Masks: Reflections on Picasso's Personality', for Picasso himself
claimed towards the end of his life:

It's the movement of painting that interests me, the dramatic movement from one effort to
the next, even if those efforts are perhaps not pushed to their ultimate end. [...] I have less
and less time, and yet I have more and more to say, and what I have to say is, increasingly,
something about what goes on in the movement of my thought. I have reached the moment,
you see, when the movement of my thought interests me more than the thought itself.[23]

Accordingly, in his introduction to *Picasso at 90: The Late Work* Bergamín
stresses the continual movement of thought as a vital creative force:

Picasso once gave the young painter Manuel Angeles Ortiz the advice to 'paint what passes
through your head without stopping to think whether it's good or bad'. [...] To the painter,
as to the poet, 'what passes through your head' means just that, as opposed to what stays
there. Art that does not pass through the head is an impossibility, but by the same token art
that stays there is equally impossible. (p. 11)

Interestingly, Juan Ramón Jiménez's championing of Bergamín's first creative
work, *El cohete y la estrella (Afirmaciones y dudas aforísticas lanzadas por
elevación)* (1923), focuses on the swift, elliptical nature of his aphoristic
writing:

Era el tercer estirón, el definitivo, para llegar con la mano a esa capa finísima, casi incolora
ya del aire, donde están las ideas inéditas. Delgado y largo de estirarse para cazar pájaros

incojibles — casi siempre. Pero él ha cojido algunos por el pecho; de otros, se ha quedado con preciosísimas plumas, o con plumas vulgares con el color del ruiseñor, de otros con la tibieza ligera de su roce, con el olor errante, con una nota caída de su fuga cantora, con la forma momentánea de su vuelo — ¡Y no es peor caza la de lo que se nos va![24]

'Una nota caída de su fuga cantora, con la forma momentánea de su vuelo', which is suggestive too in its reference to the sublime, captures Bergamín's attitude to thought, all that is worthwhile being only rarely and momentarily within reach of human expression.

Already we have a thought-cluster that surrounds the notion of exile in Bergamín's imagination: place, loss, movement; flight ('huida'), a diaspora, and the poetic flight towards the sublime ('vuelo'). The latter implies in particular a striving towards, a 'peregrinación' with all its possible manifestations. Bergamín would concur with Michael Ugarte's paraphrasing of Mazzotta in that 'to read is to be cast into exile; the search for meaning is the pilgrim's search for the sublime'.[25]

In Bergamín's estimation exile and movement are inseparable, which is why he appropriates the image of the pilgrimage for himself and his fellow Spaniards in *De una España peregrina*. The image is particularly apt since the word 'pilgrim' carries with it connotations of both solitude and solidarity, each solitary pilgrim making up part of a collectivity of pilgrims who on one level at least, that of Republicans wandering in search of lost Republican Spain, a land lost, wander together. They have a quest in common. The paradoxical nature of the pilgrim image would have appealed to Bergamín who even in 1923 believed that 'La verdadera solidaridad sólo es posible entre solitarios' (*El cohete y la estrella*, p. 82). In addition he observed that 'La animación del mundo es la solidaridad de las almas en la soledad de los cuerpos: la religión católica' (p. 97). Here solitude and solidarity are seen as characteristic of a Catholic mentality. However, later on in the same work the solitude of the poet is portrayed as the imperative that 'solidifies' or rather crystallizes thought into poetry:

El poeta va y viene de soledad a soledad: ir y venir, poético, de pensamientos. Los pensamientos solidarizan sus soledades en la soledad de la poesía como las estrellas en Dios. Soledad de soledades y todo soledad. (p. 117)

Note again the insistence upon continual, seemingly pointless movement from one 'soledad' to another, the maintenance of poetic impetus. The *movement* is what matters. That the oscillation, the implied dialectic, operates between indiscernible, undifferentiated polarities does not inhibit the impetus of the movement. On the contrary, the very sameness of the polar points appears to constitute the imperative for the continual shifting of the poet's thought, both a fascination with the oscillation and an attempted flight ('huida') from the sameness of the points of reference, solitude.

Bergamín experiences exile as solitude. The notion of solitude for Bergamín is inextricably linked with the idea of absence, pertaining, as we have already posited, to the concept of exile. In his discussion of the poetic development of the word 'soledad' from the Portuguese 'saudade', in *Lázaro, Don Juan y Segismundo*, Bergamín stresses the semantic union of absence and solitude:

Parecería que el sentimiento de la soledad se encuentra igualmente significado por estas dos palabras 'saudade' y 'soledad' en su principio. [...] 'La verdad — escribe Don Juan de Silva en esta carta — es que quieren los portugueses que la "saudade" comprenda todos los desabrimientos de la ausencia y que se componga de todos; más lo mismo digo yo de la "soledad" (¡Y mal haya el Diablo porque la conozco bien!...)'[26]

Solitude describes not only a physical state of abandonment, but more importantly a spiritual state of absence. The terrifying absence of God is nevertheless a just absence and Bergamín's sense of absence and his deliberate separation of Self from himself, the relinquishment of personal identity, is not simply an alienation which has been thrust upon him but rather a deliberate dialectical act of expulsion from Self designed to mimic the absented nature of God from the world. The negative allusions he makes to the state of his fragmented identity, when viewed from the point of view of the religious sensibility he describes in *El pozo de la angustia*, take on a new positive meaning. Again, it is the sense of loss or anguish, his desire, which propels Bergamín into his creative dialectic:

El deseo que engendra la voluntad humana es como la angustia engendradora de la ansiedad. [...] El ser está suspendido en la nada, que es el ámbito de la nada el que le afirma y verifica. ¿Ansiosamente? La existencia humana es esta suspensión del ser fuera de sí mismo, o mejor dicho, fuera de su razón, de su razón de ser frente a la nada. Porque este enfurecimiento trágico le suspende y adentra en la nada misma. Ser, para el metafísico de la angustia, como para los trágicos griegos, ¿es dejar de ser? Entrar en la nada, enterarse de ella, anonadarse. Para el pensamiento cristiano, este anonadamiento enfurecido es la afirmación de una vanidad, de un vacío que abre ansiosamente nuestro ser humano al divino.[27]

The abjection of Self, which justifies itself as an act of worship for Bergamín, is similar to Simone Weil's notion of decreation. Weil advocates a similar suspension of being, a similar distancing of Self in the act of devotion to the divine which she describes as 'attention':

Attention consists of suspending our thought, leaving it detached, empty and ready to be penetrated by the object. [...] Above all, our thought should be empty, waiting, not seeking anything, but ready to receive in its naked truth the object which is to penetrate it.[28]

Bergamín, like Weil, considers the elision of the distinction between Self and otherness to be a supreme act of generosity which ultimately becomes his salvation:

El hombre que se da a sí mismo en todo y por todo, con esa generosidad quijotesca, a fuerza de perderse en todo, todo lo encuentra; y en todo se encuentra: porque encuentra en ese entusiasmo o entrega de su ser, que a sí mismo le niega, totalmente, su afirmación o verificación humana en lo divino. El hombre no se encuentra del todo más que cuando se pierde a sí mismo. Porque encuentra a Dios.[29]

The understanding of human experience as one of exile from God requires for both Weil and Bergamín, then, the continual recognition of the pernicious influence of and illusory sense of satisfaction of the notion of individuality. Weil's purpose is analogous to Bergamín's:

It is to train the attention, to teach the attitude of intellectual waiting and to develop the capacity of the self to disappear. Thinking personally is to commit the sin of pride in 'forgetting one is God'. (p. 50)

Weil's love of God is utterly depersonalized:

Of the absent God who refuses to falsify by intervention she says 'He loves not as I love but as an emerald is green ...I too, if I were in a state of perfection, I would love as an emerald is green...I would be an impersonal person.' (p. 53)

Bergamín's love of God features the same depersonalization and is expressed in mystical terms, the consuming in fire of one's self in the divine fire:

'Unas almas se purifican al arder y otras se consumen', decía Santa Teresa. La existencia humana, al arder en tan puro fuego, consume en sí misma y por sí misma esa máscara o cobertura de su ser, como la que nos dice consumirse, al espejar el sol, la imagen de la experiencia mística de la Santa Catalina genovesa en su purgatorio: para sumirse o asumirse totalmente en su divina lumbre.[30]

Solitude is experienced as the absence of God or rather the separation from God which can only be resolved by the abandonment of one's sense of being in the world. Again, Bergamín is to take an image of utter isolation and alienation as the catalyst of the divine, of ultimate, sublime fusion.

When Bergamín describes reality, he is usually describing an inner reality, affected by external reality and created by the division he feels between external and inner reality. The divisions that also operate within his inner reality mirror and mimic his dislocation from the external world. A general atmosphere of division is something that for Pedro Salinas characterizes the modern world and modern poetry:

At the end of the first lecture we spoke of the paradisaical period of man: unity. Unity of reality and the inner world. Now we must use the word that expresses the extreme opposite: division. Modern man, this new man, is man divided, in the highest degree. [...] The two worlds are not only different but even hostile. The real world destroys the poetic world and denies it all possibility of expression. And the only grandeur that poetry still retains at this stage of the human spirit is the grandeur of complaint, the desperate cry, the magnificent revolt of the poetic world, of human illusion, against the real world.[31]

This sense of division for Salinas is intensely modern. When Bergamín describes the development of the word 'soledad' he does so within the realm of his inner reality of the spirit, which for Bergamín means within the world of poetry, his inner reality, and within the realm of Spanish literature. For Salinas, as is commonplace, inner reality is the location of the poetic soul:

For me, poetry is nothing but the aggregate of relations between this psychological reality, strange and abnormal, the poetic soul, so exceptional and clairvoyant, and external reality, usual and ordinary, the reality of the outside world. (p. 4)

It is the poetic world that Bergamín is trying to portray as the essence of his Being, and the landscape of his Being is sketched from within the world of Spanish literature as in *Lázaro, Don Juan y Segismundo,* where he exemplifies the Christian sensibility as Cervantine, as essentially 'quijotesque':

Cervantes, Góngora, Lope [...] expresaron el sentimiento de la 'soledad' de manera propia y característica. Siguiendo sus textos parecería que se nos señala cierta preferencia por su utilización plural. 'Soledades' de Góngora y 'Soliloquios' de Lope. En el romancillo famoso de *La Dorotea,* cuando el soliloquio lopista se hace soledoso de soledad, se nos dice aquello de ir y venir, de soledad a soledad, como de pensamiento a pensamiento: como si para poder andar consigo — consigo a solas — el poeta necesitase soledades y no solamente soledad.[32]

Both the Baroque and the Romantic eras of Spanish literature characterize the poet's place in the world as one of 'soledad'. 'Soledad' designates the place of the poet, and it is in the place of 'soledades' that the language of Bergamín's Being, if it is to have any meaning at all, inheres and coheres:

> Eres la luz, la verdad
> y la vida o el camino,
> porque eres la soledad.

> (*Duendecitos y coplas*, p. 26)

Bergamín situates 'soledad' as a spiritual prerequisite for the task of poetry and yet since poetry is the product of a dialectic of solitudes, the poet's purpose is being continually questioned. No one hears or understands the poet:

Mi copla se cayó al mar
y la encontró una sirena
que no la supo cantar.

(Duendecitos y coplas, p. 172)

The plurality of solitudes reflects and emphasizes the endless absence that is solitude. Only solitude itself can define solitude: Bergamín struggles with the opacity of this concept:

Es dos veces soledad
la soledad que yo tengo:
que es la soledad de estar solo
y es la soledad de estar muerto.

(Duendecitos y coplas, p. 107)

The absence that is solitude, although a place, is a place without space for the creation of criteria that would communicate the essence of solitude, that is in turn the essence of Being for the poet:

Estar vivo es no estar muerto.
Y no estar muerto es estar
solo en medio del desierto.

(Duendecitos y coplas, p. 55)

Que estés vivo o que estés muerto,
tu alma es un cielo vacío,
tu corazón un desierto.

(Duendecitos y coplas, p. 34)

No tengo más tierra que ésta:
y ésta es una tierra sola
que parece que está muerta.

(Duendecitos y coplas, p. 115)

Es tedio de la vida, es un hastío,
lo que anonada el alma en el abismo
de un solitario corazón vacío.

(Duendecitos y coplas, p. 224)

For the endless absence that is solitude affords no criteria for the communication of such extreme absence:

Yo soy farola de un mar
por el que nadie navega:
mi luz se pierde en las sombras;
y ni las sombras se enteran.   *(Duendecitos y coplas*, p. 94)

In another poem the contrast between light and dark is elided and consumed within a meaningless distinction between the void and nothingness:

> Mi pensamiento está preso
> entre el corazón y el alma;
> entre la sombra y la luz;
> entre el vacío y la nada.

(Duendecitos y coplas, p. 81)

The landscape of Being is depicted as spatial, but that space is a no-man's land; the sites of Being remain both undifferentiated from each other and, paradoxically, closed to each other, unknowable:

> Mi corazón está ciego
> y mi alma también lo está:
> con el corazón y el alma
> sólo veo oscuridad.

(Duendecitos y coplas, p. 209)

> Dime, corazón del tiempo,
> ¿has dejado de latir?
> Porque apenas si te siento.

(Duendecitos y coplas, p. 194)

In general, naming and language serve only to exacerbate the tortured sense-deprivation which for the poet is literal, figurative, and linguistic. A feature of solitude is its inexpressibility, for solitude constitutes an exile from communication, both from others and the self:

> Como el rastro de un sonido
> que tiembla en sus labios preso
> mis palabras van buscando
> las huellas de tu silencio.
>
> Mis palabras van buscando
> las huellas de tu silencio
> y encuentran la soledad
> de tu corazón desierto.
>
> Y encuentran la soledad
> de tu corazón desierto
> como el anhelo de un grito
> que está temblando en tu pecho.

(Duendecitos y coplas, p. 146)

La soledad de mi vida
se está quedando sin alma.
Mi corazón ya no tiene
sangre para poder dársela.

(*Duendecitos y coplas*, p. 32)

The intensity of solitude resides in its unicity. Such intense solitude is uttered, uncorrelative, as inexpressibility in Bergamín's poetry and such alienation can be articulated only through paradox and contradiction:

El corazón de la llama
está temblando de frío
y de sentirse tan solo,
tan oscuro y tan vacío.

(*Duendecitos y coplas*, p. 177)

Furthermore, for Bergamín only the evocation of the multiplicity and territoriality of that which is single and without place or landless can approach an expression of the anguish which is solitude. The company of solitude is solitude itself:

Solo has estado en la vida.
Solo estarás en la muerte.
Que sólo la soledad
te acompaña para siempre.

(*Duendecitos y coplas*, p. 85)

The yearning to escape isolation produces the search for company even if that company is only to be the company of other solitudes. This yearning is cosmic and by implication is otherly in the deepest sense, of the divine, for Bergamín's human solitude reflects the impersonality and absence of the divine:

También tiene miedo el mar:
tiene miedo de estar solo:
solo con su soledad.

(*Duendecitos y coplas*, p. 117)

¡Mira qué solo está el mar!
¡Qué solas están las olas
queriéndole acompañar!

(*Duendecitos y coplas*, p. 116)

> La soledad que yo tengo
> no es la soledad del mar
> ni la soledad del cielo.
>
> Yo estoy solo como el viento
> que busca pero no encuentra
> quién le dé acompañamiento.
>
> (*Duendecitos y coplas*, pp.211-12)

POETIC VOICE AND THE REALM OF THE GIFT

Just as Bergamín appropriates the voices of other great 'solitarios', for instance in his echoing of Lope in the previously cited aphorism, it is the replicating, multiplying force of solitude which paradoxically creates his only hope of company and of creativity, communication.[33]   By invoking Lope, Bergamín elaborates on the idea of multitudinous solitude.

Bergamín's glossing of other poets is entirely logical when one considers his wish to depersonalize his voice in favour of a merging with the divine. In literary terms, his highest aim is to adequately echo and mirror a desire for transcendence as it is best expressed in the voices of poetry:

La verdadera situación crítica del hombre ante el espejo no es la de contemplarse a sí mismo tan superficialmente reflejado en una imagen inexistente, es la de contemplar a los demás de ese mismo modo. Hay palabras espejos, decía Larra: son 'cristales del tiempo.'[34]

And Simone Weil reveals a similar disregard for the personality of the one who writes:

In the operation of writing, the hand which holds the pen, and the body and the soul which are attached to it, with all their social environment, are things of infinitesimal importance for those who love the truth. They are infinitely small in the order of nothingness. That at any rate is the measure of importance I attach in this operation not only to my own personality but to yours and to that of any other writer I respect. Only the personality of those whom I more or less despise matters to me in such a domain.[35]

It is the quality of the depersonalized voice which matters rather than the literary immortality of the one who writes. In his literary criticism as much as in his poetry Bergamín, as I indicated in Chapter 1, is concerned to reread and revoice the quintessential desire of man to transcend his mortal state. The power of language and in particular the language of poetry is viewed as standing apart and above individual strength. Poetic language is seen as a linguistic and divine tool of salvation, a paradoxical creator of voice, which at once denies individuality and affirms potential Being in the realm of the divine.

Solitude, an exile from all that is vital, tends to produce a schizophrenic replication of voices within the isolated Self. Voices are Bergamín's defence against the silence of his solitude. Ironically, therefore, he would, when denied a voice, commute silence to the same semantic level as speech:

> Los muertos no hablan,
> pero hasta los árboles, si los mueve el viento,
> dicen lo que callan.
>
> Nos lo están diciendo
> la hierba y las flores, la noche estrellada
> que vela su sueño.
>
> Si hablaran los muertos
> no podrían decirnos más de lo que dicen
> con tantos silencios.[36]

Words, the place of language and voices, provide the place of most effective Being:

> Dices que no te doy
> más que palabras:
> palabras volanderas
> que no son nada.
>
> Pero te engañas,
> que la palabra es aire
> y el aire es alma.
>
>   (*Poesía, VI*, p. 9)

The schizophrenic reaction expresses solitude as a lack of space, as if there were only one life for two people. Denied a sense of self, the replicating voices in poetry compensate the isolation of the exilic imagination by providing points of comparison and contrast, an illusion of definition, communication, and company. Solitude itself is divided, given less than its due space. Solitude accompanies other solitudes, accompanies itself, its mirror. Image and reality become at once indistinguishable through multiple division and the thwarted urge to calibrate fiction and reality:

> Solo has estado en la vida.
> Solo estarás en la muerte.

> Que sólo la soledad
> te acompaña para siempre.
>
> (*Duendecitos y coplas*, p. 85)

The will to express and imagine oneself as other is seen ultimately as a tragic error, for '"el delito mayor del hombre" es haber soñado' (*Duendecitos y coplas*, p. 64). Bergamín attempts to transform or metamorphose the process of his existential disintegration into the vehicle of his salvation. The notion of replication and the multiple voicing of his anguish is comparable, for instance, to his vision of time, the passing of which he combats by attempting to create an eternal moment of reality by mirroring and remirroring the present. As in the previous poem, Bergamín systematically elides the traditional divisions of past, present, and future time in order to signal the greater division of solitude. The hopeful continuum of eternity is subverted by the desolation of eternal solitude. The expansiveness of isolation, of absence, is often expressed as imprisonment; that expansiveness is sameness, continuation without sequence, repetition without growth. The unicity of solitude replicates rather than reproduces, echoes rather than replies, embodies one who is forced to live in too small a space, as if two were in the place of one, but without reply, without the other, only reflected. Only the schizophrenic voicing of this continual mirroring, repetition, replication, and echoing, only poetry, the writing out of voices, consoles and partially compensates the poet. Writing, the place of language, assuages, if only slightly, the destitution of Bergamín's non-being, his 'abismo del no ser al ser abismo / la eternidad del tiempo prisionera' (*Poesía, I*, p. 33)· He talks to himself when he says:

> Como preso en tu voz está tu llanto
> que a sollozar no ha roto,
> dándole a tus palabras más oscuro
> acento doloroso:
>
> el agua del estanque estremecida
> no deja ver su fondo,
> cuando herido su espejo transparente
> se vuelve tembloroso;
>
> deja que escape el llanto de sus prisiones,
> que las lágrimas tiemblen en tus ojos,
> aunque te quedes tú sin voz, sin alma,
> rota por el sollozo.
>
> (*Poesía, I*, p. 191)

For Bergamín, exile is the natural state of the poet. The poet´s relationship with his exile is symbiotic whilst hating his exile, he needs it for his poetry.

And poetry remains our consolation for exile, as John Berger says:

What reconciles me to my own death more than anything else is the image of a place: a place where your bones and mine are buried, thrown, uncovered, together. They are strewn there pell-mell. One of your ribs leans against my skull. A metacarpel of my left hand lies inside your pelvis. (Against my broken ribs your breast like a flower.) The hundred bones of our feet are scattered like gravel. It is strange that this image of our proximity, concerning as it does mere phosphate of calcium, should bestow a sense of peace. Yet it does. With you I can imagine a place where to be phosphate of calcium is enough.[37]

The place of restitution, then, is both a religious place of supreme generosity and an aesthetic space, the place of the sublime. The sublime in art is like religious salvation, a figuring of a desire rather than the statement of an actual experience. It is a utopian vision which is paradoxically dependent upon its impossibility for its raison d'être. Such insatiability does not undermine the desire, rather it serves only to intensify the desire and to propel the poet into a dialectics of faith which, experienced as religious, is necessarily (according to Bergamín) expressed as poetic. The poetic is the only language which can accommodate such an irrational desire to transcend, and it is in his poetry that Bergamín attempts to salvage, through language, residence in a zone which is not subject to the tyrannies of the exilic world. Like Cixous, he would have us believe that:

Everyone knows that a place exists which is not economically or politically indebted to all the vileness and compromise. That is not obliged to reproduce the system. That is writing. If there is a somewhere else that can escape the infernal repetition, it lies in that direction, where *it* writes itself, where *it* dreams, where *it* invents new worlds.[38]

Perhaps for Bergamín as for Weil *it* is 'the secret word, the word of Love who holds us in his arms from the beginning'.[39]

NOTES

1 Margaret Atwood, 'The words continue their journey', in *Interlunar* (London: Cape, 1988), p. 83.

2 A version of this chapter appears as an article in *En torno a la poesía de José Bergamín*, ed. by Nigel Dennis (Lérida: Universidad de Lleida, 1995) under the title 'La poesía exílica de José Bergamín', pp. 202-37.

3 In her essay 'Difficult Joys', in *The Body and the Text: Hélène Cixous, Reading and Teaching*, ed. by Helen Wilcox, Keith McWatters, Ann Thompson, and Linda R. Williams (New York and London: Harvester Wheatsheaf, 1990), pp. 5-30, Cixous notes: 'Exile — real or imaginary exile — presides over the destiny of writers' (p. 12). In *Three Steps on the Ladder of Writing*, trans. by Sarah Cornell and Susan Sellers (New York: Columbia University Press, 1993) Cixous observes: 'The author writes as if he or she were in a foreign country, as if he or she were a foreigner in his or her own family' (p. 20).

4 I am indebted to Hélène Cixous for many insights into the poetry of Paul Celan which I gained at her 1988 lectures at the École Internationale de Philosophie in Paris. Unfortunately, these lectures are to date

unpublished. In particular I wish to acknowledge Cixous's reading of Celan's pseudonym commented upon here and her interpretation of the poem 'Eis, Eden', a poem which I use later on in this study as a touchstone for Bergamín's poetry.

5 José Bergamín, *Calderón y cierra España y otros ensayos disparatados* (Barcelona: Planeta, 1979), p. 9.

6 John Berger, *Our Faces, my Heart, Brief as Photos* (London: Writers and Readers, 1984), p. 21.

7 As quoted by Sandra M. Gilbert, 'Introduction: A Tarantella of Theory', in Hélène Cixous and Catherine Clément, *The Newly Born Woman*, pp. ix-xviii (p. ix).

8 Mercedes Cárdenas, 'Un tema cernudiano: El poeta como ser privilegiado', *Insula*, no. 327 (February 1974), 1, 10 (p.1).

9 See George Steiner, 'Humane literacy', in George Steiner, *Language and Silence* (Harmondsworth: Penguin, 1979) pp. 21-30: 'What man has inflicted on man, in very recent time, has affected the writer's primary material — the sum and potential of human behaviour — and it presses on the brain with a new darkness' (p. 22), and Michael Hamburger's introduction to Paul Celan, *Selected Poems*, trans. by Michael Hamburger (Harmondsworth: Penguin, 1990), pp. 17-32: 'The impossibility of writing poems after Auschwitz, let alone about Auschwitz, has become a critical commonplace' (p. 22).

10 Paul Celan, *Selected Poems*, trans. by Michael Hamburger, p. 155.

11 José Bergamín, 'El disparate en la literatura española', in José Bergamín, *Al fin y al cabo (Prosas)* (Madrid: Alianza, 1981), pp. 27-57 (pp. 32-33).

12 Introduction to *Simone Weil: An Anthology*, ed. by Sïan Miles (London: Virago, 1986), pp. 1-68 (pp. 57-58).

13. See Harold Bloom, *Ruin the Sacred Truths: Poetry and Belief from the Bible to the Present Day* (Cambridge, MA: Harvard University Press, 1989), p. 3.

14 Christiane Rochefort, extract from 'Are women writers still monsters?', in *New French Feminisms*, ed. by Elaine Marks and Isabelle de Courtivron (New York and London: Harvester Wheatsheaf, 1981), pp.183-86 (p. 186).

15 Pedro Salinas, *Reality and the Poet in Spanish Poetry* (Baltimore, MD: Johns Hopkins Press, 1940), pp. 37-38.

16 See frontispiece to Paul Celan, *Selected Poems*, trans. by Michael Hamburger.

17 José Bergamín, *Duendecitos y coplas* (Santiago de Chile and Madrid: Cruz del Sur, 1963), p. 34.

18 Julia Kristeva, *Powers of Horror: An Essay on Abjection*, trans. by Leon S. Roudiez (New York: Columbia University Press, 1982), p. 8.

19 José Bergamín, 'Transparent Masks: Reflections on Picasso's Personality', in Klaus Gallwitz, *Picasso at 90: The Late Work*, ed. by Xavier Schnieper (London: Weidenfeld and Nicolson, 1971), pp. 8-26 (p. 14).

20 Quoted by Françoise Gilot in *Picasso at 90: The Late Work*, p. 188.

21 José Bergamín, *Poesía, V: Esperando la mano de nieve (1978-1981)*, (Madrid: Turner, 1985), p. 32.

22 Paul Celan, *Selected Poems*, trans. by Michael Hamburger, p. 173.

23 Quoted by Françoise Gilot in *Picasso at 90: The Late Work*, p. 166.

24 Juan Ramón Jiménez in José Bergamín, *El cohete y la estrella/La cabeza a pájaros*, p. 43.

25 Michael Ugarte, *Shifting Ground: Spanish Civil War Exile Literature* (Durham, NC and London: Duke University Press, 1989), p. 232.

26 'Romántica de soledades', in José Bergamín, *Lázaro, Don Juan y Segismundo* (Madrid: Taurus, 1959), pp. 49-66 (p. 52).

27 *El pozo de la angustia*, pp. 42-43.

28 *Simone Weil: An Anthology*, p. 8.

29 *El pozo de la angustia*, p. 44.

30 *El pozo de la angustia*, p. 44.

31 Pedro Salinas, *Reality and the Poet in Spanish Poetry*, pp. 163-64.

32 'Romántica de soledades', p. 53.

33 'El poeta va y viene de soledad a soledad: ir y venir, poético, de pensamientos. (Los pensamientos solidarizan sus soledades en la soledad de la poesía como las estrellas en Dios. Soledad de soledades y todo soledad), *El cohete y la estrella*, p. 117.

34 José Bergamín, 'Larra, peregrino en su patria', in José Bergamín, *De una España peregrina*, pp. 11-31 (p. 20).

35 *Simone Weil: An Anthology*, p. 9.

36 José Bergamín, *Poesía, VI: Canto rodado*, (Madrid: Turner, 1984), p. 29.

37 *Our Faces, my Heart, Brief as Photos*, p. 101.

[38] As quoted by Sandra M. Gilbert, in Hélène Cixous and Catherine Clément, *The Newly Born Woman*, p. ix.

[39] *Simone Weil: An Anthology*, p. 65.

CONCLUSION

At the beginning of this study I suggested that the notion of faith as a dialectical process of contact between the material world and the transcendent world informs Bergamín's religious work and his poetry. In addition, language, suffering as it does from the constraints of the material world, through its creation of objectification, militates against the ultimate purpose of that faith, which is to overcome the material and deathly nature of existence in order to merge with another transcendent world, the world of God. Language does violence to Bergamín's desire by sustaining materialism and the notion of separation as identity in this world, rather than promoting spiritual and bodily resurrection beyond it. In the first chapter I pointed out a discrepancy between the ideas of literary immortality and Christian immortality and described the first as an idea which invests heavily in a masculine, rational discourse. This discourse, as I went on to elaborate in Chapter 2, is one which, in terms of identity and art, fails to combat the problem of death for Bergamín.

Bergamín attempts to forge an alternative language in his poetry and in the third chapter I portrayed this poetry as a battle he enacts against death, where he seeks to unveil the demonic nature of language and reveal its salvationary potential in both a spiritual and bodily sense. In the following chapter I showed how such a task requires the imagination of faith in symbolic terms as a feminine principle which promotes doubt, fluidity, and confusion or merging as opposed to the rigid separations of a rational, masculine discourse. The process of salvation requires a dialectical relationship between the sacramental figure of Christ and the generative, feminine sea, as can be observed in the three sonnets. The language with which Bergamín articulates his utopian vision is one which he has reassessed in terms of human estrangement. His battle to overcome the human, Christian condition as one of exile from God involves the necessary re-engagement of the feminine. By this I mean that Bergamín exploits in his poetry those areas of language and symbolization which escape the tyranny of rational and material discourse, indulging either in the pre-rational innocence of his 'popularismo analfabetista' or in ludic, etymological reasoning in his poetry which trivializes and undermines the intellectualist rational discourse he sees as so damaging to human vision. His focus is on the realm of the gift, a supremely generous, divine realm which, sublime and utopian, yearns to escape death. This is the realm of love. In this sense the stylistics of 'popularismo' and 'barroquismo' converge in the feminine.

I suggested in Chapter 5 that love, and the image of love as all that is not divided in itself or separated from its other, acts as a utopian place towards which Bergamín's religious and aesthetic self aspires. For Bergamín, separation is a love problem and we have seen both Woman and death conflated as the muse in his poetry, both signifying estrangement for the poetic persona. Often the reader cannot say whether Bergamín addresses death or a cherished, lost lover:

> Oigo tu voz en el viento.
> La oigo en el crepitar
> de las llamas en el fuego.
>
> Me parece estarla oyendo
> como la lluvia o el agua
> que corre por el reguero.
>
> ¡Ay!, la oigo en el silencio
> de mi corazón vacío
> donde esconde su eco.

(Poesía, III, p .68)

Even in the more evidently love poetry of *La claridad desierta*, the language of solitude recalls the Romantic Sublime of a Ferrán or a Bécquer, where loss is denied against all odds, the continual figuring of a desire to merge with the absent lover:

> Estoy pensando en ti cuando no pienso
> que estoy pensando en ti, cuando quisiera
> no tener que pensar para sentirme
> de tu lejano corazón más cerca.
>
> Más cerca de esa pura lejanía
> íntimamente clara de tu ausencia:
> de ese rastro de luz que tu recuerdo:
> enciende en mí cuando de mí se aleja.

(Poesía, II, p. 16)

This poetics of loss is paradoxically affirmative, as Kathleen N. March implies:

En la poesía bergaminiana, el adjetivo *otro* sirve para diferenciar entre lo propio y lo ajeno, pero también tiene la función fundamental de indicar que lo ajeno existe porque uno posee lo suyo propio, es decir, porque es dueño de una característica o esencia cualitativamente irreductible. [...] Es esto el espacio del ser que se extiende hasta su desaparición en el no-ser, su límite.[1]

Because the poetics of loss depend upon the notion of otherness and separation, Bergamín is faced with a continual contradiction between the desire to merge with the divine and his irreducibleness. In other words, he requires an irreducible material nature from which to envisage its dissolution in the divine. In his poetry, this irreducibility or, as I previously described it, his state of estrangement and difference from God, converges repeatedly in the epistemological and linguistic problem of gender.

The sketching of Christian estrangement in terms of gender acknowledges the irreducibility of difference and separation in a permanent, undeniable, and fleshly fashion. After all, any discussion of gender assumes such difference, despite the process of denial which informs the stategies of sexual politics in the worldly, political arena. For Bergamín, at least the undeniability of difference and separation is both the thorn in the flesh of his anguish and the catalyst of his envisaged salvation. His insistence upon the figure of the mortified Christ is a testament to this. The process of mourning, desire, and resurrection, continually enacted for him in the crucifixion, depends upon the unresolved nature of the crucifixion in the world. It necessitates the prerequisite of faith, and a dialectics of faith directed always to a transcendent, unbreachable, realm and it is entirely fitting that this realm should be symbolized in terms of the feminine, from which he is epistemologically and linguistically estranged.

Thus, Bergamín's utopian vision, which is necessarily unresolved, and the dynamics of his dialectics of faith constantly claim a voice beyond his voice which holds out a promise of love and union. The voice of love is both the divine voice and the voice of poetry, a dialectics of faith which constitutes for Bergamín his 'Arte poética', his potential escape into love:

No dejes de escuchar el canto oscuro
que es cadencioso eco
de la palabra, dilatada sombra
que cobija al silencio.

Porque el 'decir de amor' de la poesía,
antes de 'trasmutar el pensamiento
en sueño', es una música que lleva
otra música dentro.

Toda forma es la forma de otra forma
que escapa de sí misma para serlo
y acompasa su paso con el paso
huidero del tiempo.

Por eso el corazón, con el latido
de la sangre, a tu verso
le da el ritmo sonoro y luminoso
de su estremecimiento.

(*Poesía, III*, p. 54)

NOTES

[1] Kathleen N. March, 'Dinámica del vacío en *La claridad desierta* de José Bergamín', *Insula*, no. 470 (May 1986), 1,14 (p. 14).

SELECT BIBLIOGRAPHY

This bibliography includes all works cited in this book as well as a number of critical studies which are directly relevant to the study of José Bergamín.

WORKS BY JOSÉ BERGAMÍN

PROSE

Aforismos de la cabeza parlante (Madrid: Turner, 1983)
Al fin y al cabo (Prosas) (Madrid: Alianza, 1981)
Al volver (Barcelona: Seix Barral, 1962)
Antes de ayer y pasado mañana (Barcelona: Seix Barral, 1974)
El arte de birlibirloque (Madrid: Turner, 1985)
El arte de birlibirloque. La estatua de don Tancredo. El mundo por montera
    (Santiago de Chile and Madrid: Cruz del Sur, 1961)
Beltenebros y otros ensayos sobre literatura española (Barcelona and Madrid:
    Noguer, 1973)
El Caballito del Diablo. El cohete y la estrella. Caracteres (Buenos Aires:
    Losada, 1942)
Calderón y cierra España y otros ensayos disparatados (Barcelona: Planeta,
    1979)
Caracteres, 2nd edn (Madrid: Turner, 1978)
La claridad del toreo (Madrid: Turner, 1985)
El clavo ardiendo, with a preface by André Malraux (Barcelona: Aymá, 1974)
Le clou brulant, with a preface by André Malraux, trans. by Jean-Claude
    Carrière (Paris: Plon, 1973)
Cristal del tiempo 1933-1983, ed. by Gonzalo Santonja (Madrid: Revolución,
    1983)
El cohete y la estrella/La cabeza a pájaros, ed. by José Esteban (Madrid:
    Cátedra, 1981)
La corteza de la letra. (Palabras desnudas) (Buenos Aires: Losada, 1957)
'Cruz y Raya': Antología, ed. by José Bergamín (Madrid: Turner, 1974)
Cruz y Raya: Revista de afirmación y negación, ed. by José Bergamín,
    (Madrid: Cruz y Raya, 1933-36)
Disparadero español I (Madrid: Cruz y Raya, 1936)
Disparadero español II (Madrid: Cruz y Raya, 1936)
Disparadero español III (Mexico DF: Séneca, 1940)

De una España peregrina, 2nd edn (Madrid: Al-Borak, 1972)

El epistolario. José Bergamín - Miguel de Unamuno (1923-1935), ed. by Nigel Dennis (Valencia: Pre-textos, 1993)

Fronteras infernales de la poesía, 2nd edn (Madrid: Taurus, 1980)

Ilustración y defensa del toreo: El arte de birlibirloque. La estatua de don Tancredo. El mundo por montera (Torremolinos: Litoral, 1974)

La importancia del demonio (y otras cosas sin importancia) (Madrid: Júcar, 1974)

Lázaro, Don Juan y Segismundo (Madrid: Taurus, 1959)

Mangas y Capirotes: España en su laberinto teatral del siglo XVII (Madrid: Ediciones del Centro, 1974)

La música callada del toreo, 3rd edn (Madrid: Turner, 1982)

El pasajero: Peregrino español en América, 3 vols (Mexico DF: Séneca, 1943)

El pensamiento de un esqueleto: Antología periodística I, ed. by Gonzalo Penalva Candela (Torremolinos: Litoral, 1984)

El pensamiento de un esqueleto: Antología periodística,II, ed. by Gonzalo Penalva Candela (Torremolinos: Litoral, 1984)

El pensamiento de un esqueleto: Antología periodística, III, ed. by Gonzalo Penalva Candela (Torremolinos: Litoral, 1984)

El pensamiento perdido: Páginas de la guerra y del destierro (Madrid: Adra, 1976)

El pozo de la angustia, 2nd edn (Barcelona: Anthropos, 1985)

Prólogos epilogales, ed. by Nigel Dennis (Valencia: Pre-textos, 1985)

'Transparent Masks: Reflections on Picasso's Personality', in Klaus Gallwitz, *Picasso at 90: The Late Work*, ed. by Xavier Schnieper (London: Weidenfeld and Nicolson, 1971), pp. 8-26

POETRY

La claridad desierta, 2nd edn (Torremolinos: Litoral, 1970)

Duendecitos y coplas (Santiago de Chile and Madrid: Cruz del Sur, 1963)

Poesía, I: Sonetos, Rimas, Del otoño y los mirlos (Madrid: Turner, 1983)

Poesía, II: La claridad desierta (Madrid: Turner, 1983)

Poesía, III: Apartada orilla (1971-1972) (Madrid: Turner, 1983)

Poesía, IV: Velado desvelo (1973-1977) (Madrid: Turner, 1983)

Poesía, V: Esperando la mano de nieve (1978-1981) (Madrid: Turner, 1985)

Poesía, VI: Canto rodado (Madrid: Turner, 1984)

Poesía, VII: Hora última (Madrid: Turner, 1984)

Poesías casi completas, 2nd edn (Madrid: Alianza, 1984)

Por debajo del sueño: Antología poética (Santiago de Chile and Madrid: Cruz del Sur, 1962)

Rimas y sonetos rezagados (Santiago de Chile and Madrid: Cruz del Sur, 1962)
X a X. Correspondencia en verso: Rafael Alberti - José Bergamín (Roma - Madrid) (Torremolinos: Litoral, 1982)

DRAMA

Don Lindo de Almería (Valencia: Pre-textos, 1988)
Enemigo que huye: Polífumo y Coloquio espiritual (1925-1926) (Madrid: Biblioteca Nueva, 1927)
Los filólogos (Madrid: Turner, 1978)
La hija de Dios y La niña guerrillera, 2nd edn (Madrid: Hispamerca, 1978)
La risa en los huesos: Tres escenas en ángulo recto y Enemigo que huye (Madrid: Nostromo, 1973)
'Tanto tienes cuanto esperas y el cielo padece fuerza o la muerte burlada', *El hijo pródigo*, no. 10 (January 1944), Acts I and II, 40-53; *El hijo pródigo*, no. 11 (February 1944), Act III and Epilogues 1 and 2, 107-19
'Los tejados de Madrid o el amor anduvo a gatas', *Primer Acto*, no. 21 (March 1961), 23-39

CRITICAL STUDIES OF JOSE BERGAMIN

BOOKS AND ARTICLES

José Bergamín, ed. by Florence Delay and Dominique Letournier (Paris: Editions du Centre Pompidou, 1989)
En torno a la poesía de José Bergamín, ed. by Nigel Dennis (Lérida: Universidad de Lleida, 1995)
Ainsa, Fernando, 'El exilio español en Uruguay: Testimonio de un "niño de la guerra"', *Cuadernos Hispanoamericanos*, nos. 473-74 (November-December 1989), 159-69
Alberti, Rafael, 'Homenaje a José Bergamín', *Primer Acto*, no. 185 (August-September 1980), 30-32
Albornoz, Aurora de, 'Para encontrarlo (José Bergamín)', *Insula*, no. 443 (October 1983), 1
_____ 'Poesía última de José Bergamín', *Insula*, no. 329 (April 1974), 4
Anderson, Andrew A., 'Las peripecias de *Poeta en Nueva York*', *Boletín de la Fundación Federico García Lorca*, 10-11 (February 1992), 97-123
Bécarud, Jean, *'Cruz y Raya' (1933-1936)* (Madrid: Taurus, 1969)
Campodonico, Luis, 'Manuel de Falla y José Bergamín: El contexto de una correspondencia', *Mundo Nuevo*, no. 25 (July 1968), 15-24

Cano, José Luis, 'La poesía de José Bergamín', *Insula*, nos. 404-05 (July-August 1980), 16-17

_____ 'En la muerte de José Bergamín', *Insula*, no. 442 (September 1983), 5

Cañizal de la Fuente, Luis, 'Beltenebros y otros ensayos...', *Insula*, no. 329 (April 1974), 4

Delay, Florence, 'La crítica citacional de José Bergamín', *Camp de l'arpa*, nos. 67-68 (September-October 1979), 15-20

Dennis, Nigel, *El aposento en el aire: Introducción a la poesía de José Bergamín* (Valencia: Pre-textos, 1983)

_____ 'Caracterología Bergaminiana', *Nueva Estafeta*, no. 3 (February 1979), 75-77

_____ 'Jorge Guillén y José Bergamín en 1927: Fragmentos de un epistolario inedito', *Revista de Occidente, no.* 144 (May 1993), 64-73

_____ 'José Bergamín (1895-1983)', *Insula*, no. 443 (October 1983), 3

_____ *José Bergamín: A Critical Introduction, 1920-1936* (Toronto, Buffalo, and London: University of Toronto Press, 1986)

_____ 'José Bergamín and the aesthetics of the Generation of 1927', *Bulletin of Hispanic Studies*, 58 (1981), 313-28

_____ 'José Bergamín, dramaturgo: Apuntes sobre la antifilología', *Cuadernos Hispanoamericanos*, no. 409 (July 1984), 111-17

_____ 'José Bergamín: Ilustración y defensa de la frivolidad', *Cuadernos Hispanoamericanos*, no. 342 (December 1978), 603-13

_____ 'José Bergamín y la exaltación del disparate', *Cuadernos Hispanoamericanos*, no. 288 (June 1974), 539-62

_____ 'José Bergamín y su "clavo ardiendo"', *Insula*, no. 341 (April 1975), 1,13

_____ 'El neobarroquismo en la prosa española de preguerra: El caso de José Bergamín', *Cuadernos Americanos*, n.s. 5 (September-October 1984),144-61

_____ *Perfume and Poison: A Study of the Relationship between José Bergamín and Juan Ramón Jiménez* (Kassel: Reichenberger, 1985)

_____ 'Posdata sobre José Bergamín: *Cruz y Raya*, una revista que habla por sí misma', *Cuadernos Hispanoamericanos*, no. 301 (July 1975), 143-59

_____ 'Rafael Alberti, José Bergamín y la Eva Gundersen de *Sobre los ángeles*', *Nueva Estafeta*, no. 15 (February 1980), 60-70

_____ 'Rafael Alberti y José Bergamín (amistad y literatura)', *Insula*, no. 379 (June 1978), 4

_____ 'La *Revista de Occidente* y *Cruz y Raya*: Ortega y Bergamín', *Revista de Occidente*, no. 72 (May 1987), 41-62

_____ '"Teatro de agitación política": El caso de José Bergamín (creación y compromiso)', *Camp de l'arpa*, nos. 67-68 (September-October 1979), 21-26

_____ 'Unamuno and Bergamín: Contexts of a Correspondence', *Revista Canadiense de Estudios Hispánicos*, 11 (1987), 257-87

Espina, Antonio, untitled review of *El cohete y la estrella*, *Revista de Occidente*, no.7 (January 1924), 125-27

Esteban, José, 'El poeta José Bergamín', *Insula*, no. 443 (October 1983), 3

Fernández Sánchez-Alarcos, Raul, 'La poesía humanizada de Bergamín y algo más sobre *Los filólogos*', *Cuadernos Hispanoamericanos*, nos. 514-15 (April-May 1993), 221-26

Garrison, David, 'Tradition and the Individual Talent of José Bergamín: *Esperando la mano de nieve*', *Hispania*, 71 (1988), 793-97

González, Juan E., 'Entrevista con José Bergamín', *Nueva Estafeta*, no. 4 (March 1979), 51-55

González Troyano, Alberto, 'Un velado desvelo para el juego de los toros', *Insula*, no. 443 (October 1983), 3

Gurméndez, Carlos, 'Bibliografía de José Bergamín', *El libro español*, no. 304 (October 1983), 52-54

Jarnés, Benjamín, 'José Bergamín: Enemigo que huye', *Camp de l'arpa*, nos. 67-68 (September-October 1979), 11

Jiménez, Juan Ramón, 'José Bergamín (1922)', in *El cohete y la estrella/La cabeza a pájaros*, ed. by José Esteban (Madrid: Cátedra, 1981), p. 43

Lacosta, Francisco C., 'Al margen de los clásicos: José Bergamín', *Hispania*, 50 (1967), 54-62

Lorenzo, María Pilar, 'La poesía analfabeta de José Bergamín', *Revue Romane*, 25 (1990), 442-53

Malraux, André, 'El clavo ardiendo', *Camp de l'arpa*, nos. 67-68 (September-October 1979), 9-10

March, Kathleen N., 'Dinámica del vacío en *La claridad desierta* de José Bergamín', *Insula*, no. 470 (May 1986), 1, 14

Maurer, Christopher, 'En torno a dos ediciones de *Poeta en Nueva York*', *Revista Canadiense de Estudios Hispánicos*, 9 (1985), 251-56

Miró, Emilio, 'La poesía de José Bergamín', *Insula*, no. 362 (January 1977), 6

Monleón, José, 'Introducción al teatro de José Bergamín', *Primer Acto*, no. 185 (August-September 1980), 25-30

Penalva Candela, Gonzalo, 'José Bergamín: Dolor de España', *Insula*, no. 469 (December 1985), 13-14

_____ *Tras las huellas de un fantasma: Aproximación a la vida y obra de José Bergamín* (Madrid: Turner, 1985)

Renart, Juan Guillermo, 'Los "Tres sonetos a Cristo crucificado ante el mar", comienzo público del Bergamín poeta', *Camp de l'arpa*, nos. 67-68 (September-October 1979), 27-33

Roullière, Yves, 'José Bergamín: L'importance du démon (1933)', *Poésie*, 47 (1988) 8-23

Roy, Claude, '¿Un retrato? Más bien, un ideograma', *Camp de l'arpa*, nos. 67-68 (September-October 1979), 13

Sabugo Abril, Amancio, 'Cruz y raya de José Bergamín', *Cuadernos Hispanoamericanos*, no. 406 (April 1984), 91-103

Salinas, Pedro, 'José Bergamín en aforismos', in *Literatura española siglo XX* (Madrid: Alianza, 1970), pp.159-64

Santos, José Alonso de, 'Presencia del teatro de Bergamín', *Primer Acto*, no. 185 (August-September 1980), 32-33

Malraux. Past, Present and Future: Conversations with Guy Saurès, ed. by Guy Saurès, trans.by Derek Coltman (London: Thames and Hudson, 1974)

Malraux, celui qui vient: (Entretiens entre André Malraux, Guy Saurès, José Bergamín), ed. by Guy Saurès (Paris: Stock, 1974).

Savater, Fernando, 'Bergamín levanta el vuelo', in *Instrucciones para olvidar el 'Quijote' y otros ensayos generales* (Madrid: Taurus, 1985), pp.195-97

Savini, Silvana, 'Tres entrevistas sobre José Bergamín', *Rassegna Iberística*, 32 (1988), 9-18 (The interviews are with Sabina de la Cruz, Carlos Gurméndez, and Mario Vargas Llosa)

Antología del humor negro español: Del Lazarillo a Bergamín, ed. by Cristóbal Serra (Barcelona: Tusquets, 1976)

Suñén, Luis, 'La reflexión creadora de José Bergamín', *Cuadernos Hispanoamericanos*, no. 297 (March 1975), 681-84

Zambrano, María, 'José Bergamín', *Camp de l'arpa*, nos. 67-68 (September-October 1979), 7

UNPUBLISHED WORK

Dennis, Nigel, '*Popularismo y barroquismo* in the Work of José Bergamín' (unpublished doctoral thesis, University of Cambridge, 1976)

OTHER WORKS CITED

Atwood, Margaret, *Interlunar* (London: Cape, 1988)

Berdyaev, Nicolas, *Slavery and Freedom* (London: Bles, 1943)

Berger, John, *Our Faces, my Heart, Brief as Photos* (London: Writers and Readers, 1984)

Bloom, Harold, 'Poetic Origins and Final Phases', in *Modern Criticism and Theory*, ed. by David Lodge (London and New York: Longman, 1988), pp. 241-52

_____ *Ruin the Sacred Truths: Poetry and Belief from the Bible to the Present Day*, (Cambridge, MA: Harvard University Press, 1989)

Braidotti, Rosi, 'The Politics of Ontological Difference', in *Between Feminism and Psychoanalysis*, ed. by Teresa Brennan (London and New York: Routledge, 1989), pp. 89-105

Bruns, Gerald L., *Modern Poetry and the Idea of Language* (New Haven, CT: Yale University Press, 1974)

Campbell, Joseph, with Bill Moyers, *The Power of Myth*, ed. by Betty Sue Flowers (New York: Doubleday, 1988)

Cárdenas, Mercedes, 'Un tema cernudiano: El poeta como ser privilegiado', *Insula*, no. 327 (February 1974), 1,10

Celan, Paul, *Selected Poems*, trans. by Michael Hamburger (Harmondsworth: Penguin, 1990)

Cixous, Hélène, and Catherine Clément, *The Newly Born Woman*, trans. by Betsy Wing, Theory and History of Literature, 24 (Manchester: Manchester University Press, 1986)

Cixous, Hélène, 'Difficult Joys', in *The Body and the Text: Hélène Cixous. Reading and Teaching*, ed. by Helen Wilcox, Keith McWatters, Ann Thompson, and Linda R. Williams (New York and London: Harvester Wheatsheaf, 1990), pp. 5-30

_____, *Three Steps on the Ladder of Writing*, trans. by Sarah Cornell and Susan Sellers (New York: Columbia University Press, 1993)

Curtis, David, 'Marx against the Marxists: Catholic Uses of the Young Marx in the *Front Populaire* Period (1934-1938)', *French Cultural Studies*, 2 (1991), 165-81

Evans, Jo, 'Carmen Conde's *Mujer sin Edén*: Controversial notions of "sin"', in *Women Writers in Twentieth-century Spain and Spanish America*, ed. by Catherine Davies (Lewiston, MD: Mellen, 1993), pp. 71-83

The Feminist Critique of Language: A Reader, ed. by Deborah Cameron (London and New York: Routledge, 1989)

Freud, Sigmund, 'Beyond the Pleasure Principle', in Sigmund Freud, *The Essentials of Psycho-Analysis* (London: Hogarth Press and the Institute of Pyscho-analysis, 1986), pp. 218-67

Fried, Debra, 'Rhyme Puns', in *On Puns: The Foundation of Letters*, ed. by Jonathan Culler (Oxford: Blackwell, 1988), pp. 83-99

Guillén, Jorge, 'Apéndice: Lenguaje de poema, una generación', in Jorge Guillén, *Lenguaje y poesía*, 3rd edn (Madrid: Alianza, 1983), pp. 181-97

Havard, Robert G., *From Romanticism to Surrealism: Seven Spanish Poets* (Cardiff: University of Wales Press, 1988)

Kafka, Franz, *The Diaries of Franz Kafka 1910-1923*, ed. by Max Brod (Harmondsworth: Penguin, 1972)

Kristeva, Julia, 'On the Melancholic Imaginary', in *Discourse in Psychoanalysis and Literature*, ed. by Shlomith Rimmon-Kenan (London: Methuen, 1987), pp. 104-23

_____ *Powers of Horror: An Essay on Abjection*, trans. by Leon S. Roudiez (New York: Columbia University Press, 1982)

_____ 'Women's Time?', in *The Kristeva Reader*, ed. by Toril Moi (Oxford: Blackwell, 1986), pp.186-213

Maritain, Jacques, '¿Quién pone puertas al canto?', *Cruz y Raya* (April 1935), reprinted in *'Cruz y Raya': Antología*, ed. by José Bergamín (Madrid: Turner, 1974), pp. 295-316

Meltzer, Françoise, 'Eat Your *Dasein*: Lacan's Self-Consuming Puns', in *On Puns: The Foundation of Letters*, ed. by Jonathan Culler (Oxford: Blackwell, 1988), pp. 156-63.

Moi, Toril, *Sexual/Textual Politics: Feminist Literary Theory* (London and New York: Methuen, 1985)

Ortega y Gasset, J., *Obras completas*, 4th edn, 10 vols (Madrid: Revista de Occidente, 1957-58)

Paz, Octavio, *Conjunctions and Disjunctions*, trans. by Helen Lane (New York: Arcade Publishing, 1990)

Revilla, Alejo, 'El Cristianismo y los misterios del mundo greco-romano', in *Cruz y Raya*, 15 April 1933, 67-99

Rochefort, Christiane, 'Are Women Writers Still Monsters?', in *New French Feminisms*, ed. by Elaine Marks and Isabelle de Courtivron (New York and London: Harvester Wheatsheaf, 1980), pp. 183-86

Ronell, Avital, *'The Sujet Suppositaire*: Freud and Rat Man', in *On Puns: The Foundation of Letters*, ed. by Jonathan Culler (Oxford: Blackwell, 1988), pp. 115-39

Sahuquillo, Angel, *Federico García Lorca y la cultura de la homosexualidad: Lorca, Dalí, Cernuda, Gil-Albert, Pardos y la voz silenciada del amor homosexual* (Stockholm: Stockholms Universtet, 1986)

Saïd, Edward W., 'The Text, the World, the Critic', in *Textual Strategies: Perspectives in Post-Structural Criticism*, ed. by Josué V. Harari (London: Methuen, 1980), pp. 161-88

Salinas, Pedro, *Reality and the Poet in Spanish Poetry* (Baltimore, MD: Johns Hopkins Press, 1940)

_____ 'El signo de la literatura española del siglo XX', in Pedro Salinas, *Literatura española siglo XX* (Madrid: Alianza, 1983), pp. 34-45

Steiner, George, 'Humane literacy', in George Steiner, *Language and Silence: Essays 1958-1966* (Harmondsworth: Penguin, 1979), pp. 21-30

_____ *Real Presences* (London and Boston, MA: Faber, 1989)

Storr, Anthony, *Solitude* (London: Flamingo, 1989)

Ugarte, Michael, *Shifting Ground: Spanish Civil War Exile Literature* (Durham, NC and London: Duke University Press, 1989)

Unamuno, Miguel de, *La agonía del cristianismo*, 2nd edn (Madrid: Alianza, 1986)

_____ *Del sentimiento trágico de la vida*, 2nd edn (Madrid: Espasa Calpe, 1980)

Weil, Simone, *Simone Weil: An Anthology*, with an introduction by Sïan Miles (London: Virago, 1986)

Wittgenstein, Ludwig, *Tractatus Logico-Philosophicus*, trans. by D.F. Pears and B.F. McGuinness, with an introduction by Bertrand Russell (London and Henley: Routledge and Kegan Paul, 1974)

Wyly, James, *The Phallic Quest: Priapus and Masculine Inflation* (Toronto: Inner City Books, 1989)

INDEX OF WORKS BY JOSÉ BERGAMÍN

THE POETRY OF JOSÉ BERGAMÍN
INDEX OF FIRST LINES

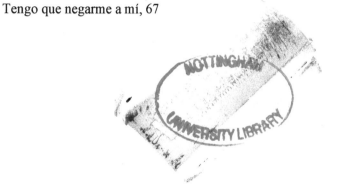